Latvians in Michigan

Discovering the Peoples of Michigan is a series of publications examining the state's rich multicultural heritage. The series makes available an interesting, affordable, and varied collection of books that enables students and lay readers to explore Michigan's ethnic dynamics. A knowledge of the state's rapidly changing multicultural history has far-reaching implications for human relations, education, public policy, and planning. We believe that Discovering the Peoples of Michigan will enhance understanding of the unique contributions that diverse and often unrecognized communities have made to Michigan's history and culture.

Latvians in Michigan

Silvija D. Meija

Michigan State University Press

East Lansing

♾ The paper used in this publication meets the minimum requirements
of ANSI/NISO Z39.48-1992 (R 1997) (Permanence of Paper).

Michigan State University Press
East Lansing, Michigan 48823-5245

Printed and bound in the United States of America.
12 11 10 09 08 07 06 05   1 2 3 4 5 6 7 8 9 10

LIBRARY OF CONGRESS CATALOGING-IN-PUBLICATION DATA
Meija, Silvija D.
Latvians in Michigan / Silvija D. Meija.
p. cm. — (Discovering the peoples of Michigan)
Includes bibliographical references and index.
ISBN 0-87013-754-9 (pbk. : alk. paper)
1. Latvian Americans—Michigan—History. 2. Immigrants—Michigan—History.
3. Latvian Americans—Michigan—Social conditions. 4. Michigan—Ethnic relations.
5. Michigan—Social conditions. I. Title. II. Series.
F575.L4M45 2005
977.4'0049193—dc22
2005014302

Cover design by Ariana Grabec-Dingman
Book design by Sharp Des!gns, Lansing, Michigan
Cover photo: Latvian children folk dancing. Photo by S. Meija.

Michigan State University Press is a member of the Green Press Initiative and is
committed to developing and encouraging ecologically responsible publishing
practices. For more information about the Green Press Initiative and the use of
recycled paper in book publishing, please visit *www.greenpressinitiative.org.*

Visit Michigan State University Press on the World Wide Web at
www.msupress.msu.edu

To Ilze, Anna, and Janis

ACKNOWLEDGMENTS

I gratefully thank the many people for their unfailing kindness and assistance. They provided pictures, books, pamphlets, personal writings and other information. Also, many people gave interviews and spent countless hours editing the book. Their research, observations and insight were often critical. My sincere appreciation and gratitude to all of you!

SERIES ACKNOWLEDGMENTS

Discovering the Peoples of Michigan is a series of publications that resulted from the cooperation and effort of many individuals. The people recognized here are not a complete representation, for the list of contributors is too numerous to mention. However, credit must be given to Jeffrey Bonevich, who worked tirelessly with me on contacting people as well as researching and organizing material.

The initial idea for this project came from Mary Erwin, but I must thank Fred Bohm, director of the Michigan State University Press, for seeing the need for this project, for giving it his strong support, and for making publication possible. Also, the tireless efforts of Keith Widder and Elizabeth Demers, senior editors at Michigan State University Press, were vital in bringing DPOM to fruition.

Otto Feinstein and Germaine Strobel of the Michigan Ethnic Heritage Studies Center patiently and willingly provided names for contributors and constantly gave this project their tireless support. Yvonne Lockwood of the Michigan State University Museum has also suggested and advised contributors.

Many of the maps in the series were prepared by Gregory Anderson at the Geographical Information Center (GIS) at Western Michigan University under the directorship of David Dickason. Additional maps have been contributed by Ellen White.

Other authors and organizations provided comments on other aspects of the work. There are many people that were interviewed by the various authors who will remain anonymous. However, they have enabled the story of their group to be told. Unfortunately, their names are not available, but we are grateful for their cooperation.

Most of all, this work is a tribute to the writers who patiently gave their time to write and share their research findings. Their contributions are noted and appreciated. To them goes most of the gratitude.

ARTHUR W. HELWEG, *Series Co-editor*

Contents

Introduction

Latvians in Michigan have contributed to the culture and economy of
the state far more than their numbers might suggest. This book will
examine Latvia in the context of its location in Europe and give a
brief history of the country. We will see how World War II culminated in
famine, death, and eventual flight by many Latvian refugees from their
homeland. Most Latvian emigrants eventually made their way after the
war to Sweden or Germany, where they lived in various displaced persons camps. From there they were sponsored by individuals or organizations and immigrated to various parts of the world. Many immigrated
to the United States, where they established new roots and tried to perpetuate their cultural heritage while establishing new lives.

Over five thousand Latvians found their way to Michigan in the late
1940s and early 1950s. They found gainful employment, purchased
homes, and became an integral part of the Michigan population. They
added to the labor force by working in a multitude of fields and positions. Most sought to reeducate themselves and struggled to educate
their children in the state's many fine colleges and universities. In study-
ing the different ethnic populations of the state, one can see that dis-
tinctive cultural patterns exist in Michigan; there is a cultural mosaic.
Each ethnic group, including the Latvians, is marked by characteristic

histories and customs and does not stand in isolation but exists as part of a larger political whole.[1] Dr. Jack Glazier, who has done extensive anthropological research, states that culture, history, and language represent compelling group emblems that motivate action and solidify a particular community, while distinguishing it from all others.[2]

What stands out in the Latvians' attempts to establish a new life in Michigan was their quest to maintain their cultural identity while coexisting in a larger community. For the first ten years or so after the development of the Latvian communities in Michigan, this struggle was founded on the desire to perpetuate all aspects of Latvian culture, as many felt that the time would eventually come when they would return to a free homeland. They worried that by the time this happened, communist rule would have stifled and desecrated the Latvian cultural identity. Thus, those who returned to their native land would need to bring with them the preserved heritage of their country, to instill and redevelop a flourishing economy and rich cultural identity.

In the 1950s and 1960s Latvians participated vigorously in Captive Nations endeavors, working to show Michigan residents, as well as the world, that they had not forgotten their homeland and were working to free those who were imprisoned by communism. Captive Nations week was established by a joint resolution of the Eighty-sixth Congress on 17 July, 1959 as a U.S. public law. The purpose was to bring to attention that there are many people across the globe who are enslaved by oppressive governments and deserve to be liberated and live in freedom.

An underlying goal of Latvians in Michigan as well as other parts of the United States and Canada is to maintain their language and culture. However, the fact is that the number of Latvians in Michigan, as well as in other parts of the country is dwindling. Assimilation by intermarriage is a fact, though many couples have chosen to teach their children the language and integrate them into Latvian society, even though one parent does not speak the language. For example, my son was playing with a friend at the Latvian Center Garezers. Both boys were around eight or nine years old. I was visiting with the boy's father, who is not Latvian. I was pleasantly surprised when he excused himself, went into the house where the boys were playing, and told his son to speak Latvian. Coming out, he commented that his greatest joy would be to

Coming to America

I remember being seven years old. Together with my parents and grandparents, we lived in a displaced persons camp in Germany for four years. We finally found sponsors in upstate New York and were put on a refurbished cargo ship, making our way across the Atlantic to our new home in America. I remember running on the deck with the other boys and playing with small children.

There was great excitement, for we were a day away from New York harbor. My grandfather, who was in his late seventies, was walking on the upper deck. He fell on the slick surface and was knocked unconscious, but within a few hours was able to walk. He had lost his memory but my parents thought it was a temporary thing.

We first saw the massive city and then the Statue of Liberty came into view. The ship docked at Ellis Island, where immigrants were to be processed. I remember the long lines, the commotion, and my parents' great anticipation. Our family went through the screening process where papers were checked and physical examinations were given; everything went fine until my grandfather was questioned through a translator. He did not know his name, his wife's name, or where he had landed. He was led to another room for questioning.

Eventually, we all had to leave Ellis Island, except for my grandfather, who was not given permission to enter the United States. He was kept there for a week and then returned to Germany. He was placed in a nursing home, where he eventually died. We never saw his smiling face again. Our family traveled to our new home in upstate New York. My mother and grandmother were devastated, not knowing what had happened to my grandfather. Mother, who spoke English, wrote many letters to officials trying to get information about his condition and perhaps gain passage for him to America. However, it was clear that invalids and those with medical problems would not be accepted. Grandfather was so close to his new home, but he never saw it. He was in the shadow of the Statue of Liberty, the symbol of freedom and a new beginning, only to have the shadow cast on his back as he was taken away.

instill the language and culture of his wife's ancestors in his children. We can see that in spite of intermarriage, cultural retention is possible.

The process by which Latvians established new lives in Michigan is the same as that by which they established themselves in many other parts of the United States, and in Canada, Australia, England, and South America. The struggle to find new jobs, develop new professions, reeducate themselves, and become a part of the larger community, while still maintaining their cultural identity was common throughout the Latvian immigrant community

In 1991 Latvia gained independence and a new government was formed. Perhaps there is therefore no longer a need for Latvians in America to preserve their cultural heritage, because those who desire to return to their native soil can now do so. However, the need to instill cultural identity and pride in one's heritage in the next generation is still prevalent today in many Latvian communities, despite the fact that Latvia is now free from Soviet domination. Even in the twenty-first century, Latvians in Michigan, and in other parts of the world, continue to explore their need to find meaning in their culture. "It has been a nearly insurmountable challenge to many ethnic groups, recognizing that a quest for education, economic improvement, social mobility—in short the pursuit of particular goals enshrined in the American value system—would bring heavy costs to the cause of ethnic community."[3] The Latvian population is now dealing with these challenges; most first- and second-generation Latvian Americans have learned how to balance their daily lives in a "cultural mosaic" and continue to work to instill their cultural heritage in their children.

Immigrants from countries such as Ireland, Italy, Finland, and so on have come to Michigan over the past century seeking economic improvement. Men usually came and found jobs, sending money back to the homeland. Some would eventually save money and return home, while others sent for their families, and one by one would transport everyone to the new land. Also, these ethnic groups came in greater numbers. Immigrants who came to Michigan after World War II were mostly from Poland, Lithuania, the Ukraine, Estonia and Latvia. These ethnic groups' homelands had been taken and they were political refugees. They did not come of their own free will, but were forced to seek and establish a life in a new land.

There are three large Latvian communities in Michigan, in Kalamazoo, Detroit, and Grand Rapids, with several smaller enclaves elsewhere in the state. We shall look at how the first immigrants chose the particular region in which they would settle, how they helped others to settle in their communities, and how they established cultural and ethnic unity while living in their new homeland. Moreover, we will examine the ways in which Latvians today are taking part in, thriving in, and adding to the Michigan culture and economy, and will document the relationships that have been established with Latvia since 1991.

Latvia: Its Location and History

Latvia is located on the eastern coast of the Baltic Sea. It shares borders with Estonia, Russia, Belarus, and Lithuania. Its land area of about 25,000 square miles could be compared to that of Michigan's Upper Peninsula. It is divided into four districts: Latgale, Kurzeme, Vidzeme, and Zemgale. The land is mostly flat, though it features a number of beautiful river valleys and numerous lakes and marshes. Forests cover about 41 percent of Latvia's territory. The climate also can be compared to that of Michigan's Lower Peninsula.[4]

The first known human settlement in the territory that is now Latvia took place soon after the end of the Ice Age, at approximately 9000 BCE. By 2000 BCE the territory was the northernmost settlement of the Baltic ethnic groups. Baltic and Finno-Ugric tribes mingled in the area, and extensive migration led to the Balts becoming the dominant group in the area.[5]

At the beginning of the twelfth century, the independent development of communities on the eastern coast of the Baltic Sea was interrupted by the arrival of western Europeans, mainly German Christian crusaders who came east to spread the Catholic faith. After a struggle, which lasted many years, the crusaders succeeded in establishing the Livonian state in the territory of present-day Latvia and Estonia. Livonia

Map 1. Latvia in Europe.

was a political union of territories belonging to the Livonian Order of Knights and the Catholic Church. Its territory stretched over the home-lands of several Baltic tribes. There developed a political and economic unity within the Livonian Order, which eventually stimulated the unification of the local tribes into one Latvian linguistic community.[6]

The Livonian Wars (1558-83) began as Muscovite Russia's attempt to conquer Livonia led to Latvia's partition by Sweden and the Grand Duchy of Poland-Lithuania. The Duchy of Kurzeme (Curland), a semi-independent state paying tribute to Poland, became so successful in the seventeenth century that it held colonies in Africa and on the Caribbean island of Tobago, where people with Latvian or semi-Latvian surnames can still be found today.[7]

The new wave of Russian expansion began in 1700 and in 1795 led to the complete incorporation of the lands on the eastern shore of the Baltic Sea into the Russian empire. The privileged conditions of the largely German landed gentry did not suffer any particular ills under Polish, Swedish, or Russian rule.[8] They continued to subjugate the Latvian serfs, putting them to work on large farms, thus keeping the population in servitude.

The Latvian National Identity Emerges

The Latvians began to consider themselves a separate nation in the first part of the nineteenth century, when the first Latvian-language newspapers were published. The Latvian intelligentsia, especially a group calling itself the "Young Latvians," did a great deal to develop the Latvian literary language and Latvian culture. Threatened by this quest for a national identity, beginning in the 1880s the Russian government began a program of deliberate Russification in the Baltic provinces.[9] All aspects of culture, religion, education, and business were mandated to use the Russian language.

The demand for Latvian national independence became prevalent in the early years of the twentieth century. The revolution of 1905-7 was, in Latvia, an outright struggle against German landowners and the Russian policy of national oppression. The second year of World War I crippled most of the country. As the German army occupied the western half, one-fifth of Latvia's 2.5 million inhabitants became refugees, and most of Latvia's industry was moved to Russia. In order to fight against the German onslaught, Latvian volunteer battalions were formed in July 1915. By 1916 the Latvian Riflemen's force had expanded to eight regiments, with a total of forty thousand soldiers. They succeeded in temporarily halting the German takeover, but after the February revolution of 1917 in Russia, the Latvian Riflemen Strēlnieki, whose founder was Jānis Goldmanis, were disappointed by mediocre Russian military leadership and were enticed by the radical social and national programs of the Bolsheviks.[10]

In 1918, at the end of World War I, German troops began withdrawing from Latvia. The people regarded the Riflemen and the Latvian

Bolsheviks, led by Peteris Stucka, as liberators. The provisional government, headed by Karlis Ulmanis, proclaimed Latvia an independent republic on November 18, 1918. However, the brutal tactics of the Bolsheviks, as well as the famine resulting from their socialist policies, soon turned the Latvian people against them. About half of the Riflemen deserted to the provisional government. In 1918 the overwhelming majority among Latvia's inhabitants supported the new, independent state.[11]

Yet Latvia's German gentry, the wealthy landowners as well as the German volunteers supporting them, wanted to see a pro-German government in Latvia. In April 1919, there was a coup attempt against the Ulmanis government, and in October of the same year, an attempt was made to occupy the territory controlled by the provisional government. On November 11, 1919, however, the German troops were defeated and were soon driven out of Latvia.[12]

Prosperity between the World Wars

Despite the loss of the greater part of its industry and one-quarter of its population, the new Latvian state began to flourish economically, once the struggle for independence had ended. By the end of the 1920s, the nation had reached living standards comparable to those of Western Europe. The most significant political achievement was the agrarian reform, which granted land to almost 145,000 landless peasants and guaranteed the new nation's social and economic stability. Latvia set an example with its approach to minority rights, guaranteeing ethnic minorities, who comprise one-quarter of Latvia's population, full cultural and educational rights.[13] Extensive educational reforms also took place at this time, and the country had the most educated populace per capita in all Europe. During this time of economic development the Minox camera, known as the "spy camera," was invented. The Minox camera was the creation of a gifted technical designer, Walter Zapp, in 1936. Full production began in 1938 at the Valsts Electrotechniskā Fabrībka. After the war in 1945, the manufacturing was resumed by Mr. Zapp in cooperation with a German company call GmbH. Today it is produced by E. Leitz company in Wetzlar,

Germany. Latvia also became known throughout Europe at this time as a major exporter of dairy products, bacon, and forest products. This was a time of tremendous social and economic growth, and national pride was boundless.

An extensive economic and political crisis developed during the 1930s that was caused by parliamentary corruption and frequent changes in the government. Reform plans were developed, but political and economic unrest was inevitable. On May 15, 1934, Kārlis Ulmanis and his supporters staged a bloodless coup and established an authoritarian dictatorship in Latvia.[14] President Ulmanis felt that this was the only way to lead the country into political stability, unity, and continuing economic and social progress.

The outbreak of World War II found Latvia unprepared to fight off German or Russian dominance, and relying on its self-declared neutrality was not enough. The lack of a tight military and political union with the other Baltic States, Poland, or other Western nations prevented Latvia from averting the destruction planned for it by the Soviet-German Molotov-Ribbentrop Pact signed on August 23, 1939. In October 1939, the Soviet Union forced Latvia to allow troops into Latvian territory, and by June 17, 1940, the Soviets occupied the country completely. The Latvian government considered military resistance futile and succumbed to the takeover.[15] A small, flourishing country, because of its geographic location on the Baltic Sea, Latvia had historically been at the mercy of giant, imperialist nations. The port in Riga, the capitol, was the most northern port that did not freeze in the winter. This only added to the desirability of controlling the Latvian nation.

The Communist Takeover

A puppet government, at first without any Communists, was established under the leadership of Augusts Kirhensteins. President Ulmanis was allowed to remain in the position of president for another month. Hoping to save his nation from even greater misery, President Ulmanis signed all decrees dictated to him by Moscow. However, the attempt to appease Moscow proved futile and Latvia was annexed into the Soviet Union. A period thereafter known as the "Year of Terror" followed.[16]

The Red Terror

As Dr. Modris Eksteins states in his book, *Walking Since Daybreak:* "Arrests came at night. Prisoners were crammed into cells. Interrogations were brutal affairs. The only options allowed a prisoner were, as one survivor put it 'admit or confess.' In an article published during the strife after the First World War, a Latvian Communist had given advice for interrogations: 'Do not ask for incriminating evidence to prove that the prisoner opposed the Soviet either by arms or by word. Your first duty is to ask him what class he belongs to, what were his origins, education, and occupation. These questions should decide the fate of the prisoner. This is the meaning and essence of Red Terror'" (118).

On the night of June 13-14, 1941, the Soviets deported approximately 20,700 civilians, including children and the elderly, to Siberia.[17] The Soviets had developed lists of Latvians who they felt were a threat to their power; government officials, ministers, professionals in many fields, as well as those who had spoken against the new regime. In the middle of the night homes were stormed by armed soldiers; men, women, and children were dragged out in their bedclothes, taken in trucks to railway stations, and put in cattle cars to be transported. The Soviets had lists of "alleged" traitors and those working against their regime. The "banging black boot" in the middle of the night sent chills throughout the population. This night remains a deep-rooted memory for many Latvians as the epitome of barbarism and brutality against a peace-loving nation. Over several years, people simply disappeared; their fate was to be shipped to Siberia or killed by the secret police.[18]

In 1941 the Soviets began to nationalize trade and industry, but the German invasion and eventual occupation of Latvia in the summer of that year interrupted their program. The Germans did not return Soviet nationalized property to their rightful owners, except land in the countryside and some homes in the cities. The Germans took advantage of the extensive anti-Communist and anti-Russian sentiment created by the Year of Terror to recruit Latvians for German military units. On February 10, 1943, by direct orders from Hitler, a general mobilization was instituted, which established a separate legion of the SS-Waffen troops, known as the Latvian Legion (Latvijas Leǵions).[19] It should be noted that most young men were drafted and had no choice but to serve under the insignia of Germany.

The Central Council of Latvia led a significant resistance movement against the German occupation. This group maintained contacts with Sweden, sent documentation of Nazi atrocities to Western allies, and organized the transportation of refugees to Sweden. Pushed back by a Soviet re-invasion, the German army in western Latvia (Kurzeme) surrendered on May 8, 1945. Some 130,000 Latvian refugees fled, by land and sea, mostly to Sweden and Germany, along with the withdrawing German army.[20] This massive exodus took place because many Latvians feared that under the Russian regime they would again face deportation to Siberia or death (and thousands were indeed deported or killed). Most felt that this emigration was temporary; the war would end and they would return to a free homeland to begin life anew. My mother told me that her family had to leave most of their worldly possessions, taking only what they could carry. Yet they locked the apartment door in Riga to await their eventual return. Also, once my parents saw that the Soviet occupation was imminent, they buried (as did many Latvians) silver and crystal pieces in large barrels at their parents' farm. Again, most planned to return to claim their rightful possessions. However, world powers had other intentions, and such a return would not be possible for almost fifty years, until the fall of the Soviet Union.

The Iron Curtain Descends

As the Red Army occupied Latvia for a second time, Sovietization began again.[21] The socialization of the national economy was completed with the collectivization of agriculture. Privately owned land was taken away, and people were forced to live and work in state-owned farms and industries. For example, a farmer who had owned many acres of land and run a prosperous farming operation was left with nothing. All land was confiscated and eventually his home was taken. He and his family were placed in one of the collective apartment buildings that sprouted up throughout the countryside, living in a set living space (a certain square footage was allowed per person). The era of collectivization had begun. By 1953, some 120,000 people had been killed, imprisoned, or deported. The "curtain" was down and none could escape. A proud, hardworking, nationalistic, and culturally rich people had been brought to near annihilation. Those who posed any threat to the new regime were either deported or killed. People could no longer walk with their heads held high, but were relegated to acting as though they were invisible, like shadows, walking with downcast and averted eyes. They were afraid to look anyone in the eyes for fear that they would be arrested for a trumped up charge at the mercy of the occupiers. Terror that would blanket the nation for many years had been implanted.

The Soviet Union also instituted a policy of Russification. Intensive industrialization of the country demanded extra labor. This led to the importation of 750,000 Russian "immigrants." By 1989 the flood of outsiders had lowered the percentage of indigenous Latvians living in the country to as little as 52 percent of the total population. The Russian language dominated both public and private life. An attempt by Latvian Nationalist Communists in 1959 to reverse the trend was suppressed, as were individual dissidents active throughout the occupation.[22] A small country, unable to defend itself with its honest and hardworking people, had been engulfed by the Communist regime.

Open discussion of the effects of Sovietization and Russification began only after the implementation of Mikhail Gorbachev's policies of glasnost and perestroika in 1985. The first open opposition organizations, Helsinki-86 and the Environmental Protection Club, were established in 1986-87 with the aim of protecting human rights and the desecrated environment. Mass rallies took place at the Freedom Monument in Riga on June 14 and August 23, 1987, although countless other rallies were crushed by security forces.[23]

A Ray of Hope: The Restoration of Independence

The Latvian Popular Front (LPF) was a group of individuals who called for an end to the totalitarian regime in Latvia. The front held its first congress in October 1988. It boasted two hundred thousand members and soon became the greatest political force in Latvia at that time. The majority of participants wanted a reformed communist authority with expanded political and economic autonomy for the Latvian Soviet Socialist Republic. A second, more determinedly pro-independence organization, the Latvian National Independence Movement, was established in 1988. As the idea of Latvian independence gained increasing support among the population, the LPF also called for the full independence of Latvia.[24]

August 23, 1989, marked the fiftieth anniversary of the Soviet-German pact that assigned the Baltic states to the Soviet "sphere of influence" and directly led to the Soviet occupation of the Baltics. That day an estimated two million Baltic residents formed an unbroken human chain from the Lithuanian capital of Vilnius, through the Latvian capital of Riga, to the Estonian capitol of Tallinn. This demonstration was called the "Baltic Way."[25] The intent was to show the Soviet regime that the populace was demanding autonomy.

During this time the residents were split into loose groups either supporting or opposing independence. The Latvian Communist Party and its satellite organizations headed the opponents of independence. Most of these people were Soviet military veterans and non-Latvians who immigrated or were sent to Latvia after World War II. There were also those who advocated seeking independence within the confines of the Soviet and Soviet-Latvian constitutions, to avoid military or economic retaliation by the Soviet Union.[26] One must keep in mind that history had shown Latvia always to be at the mercy of a domineering, militaristic power. Latvians had been killed, deported, and "Russified" for two generations; the potential brutality was a real and constant threat. The Soviet Latvian Supreme Council (parliament) proclaimed independence for Latvia on May 4, 1990, and a transition period was announced pending restoration of national authority.[27] The Satversme (Constitution) of 1922 was partially restored, but parts of the Soviet Latvian Constitution, as well as the Soviet Latvian criminal and civil codes, were declared to remain in effect pending revisions. Anatolijs Gorbunovs, a former ideological secretary of the Latvian Communist Party, was chosen chairman of parliament and thus head of state. Ivars Godmanis, the chairman of the LPF political committee, was elected prime minister.[28]

On January 2, 1991, the "black beret" paratroop force was ordered by the Communist Party leadership to occupy the building in which nearly all of Latvia's newspapers and magazines were published. This occupation continued until the collapse of the Soviet coup attempt in August 1991.[29] Throughout early 1991, Latvian customs points were attacked, often bloodily, by the Soviet "black berets," and numerous explosions were detonated in Riga. On January 20, 1991, the "black berets" attacked the Latvian Interior Ministry. Five people, including a well-known Latvian film producer, his cameraman, two police officers, and a passerby, were killed in the gunfire.[30] Yet the long-suppressed nation had tasted freedom; a few rays of potential independence had flickered on the stifled people. There was no turning back.

A New Beginning

On August 21, 1991, the Supreme Council adopted a resolution on the full restoration of Latvian state authority. In late 1992 the Supreme Council proclaimed elections to the first post-independence Latvian parliament, or Saeima, which were held on June 5 and 6, 1993.[31] The convening of the fifth Saeima after the elections in July was the last step in restoring the political independence of Latvia. On July 7, 1993, Guntis Ulmanis, representing the Latvian Farmer's Union Party, was elected president.[32] This position was a three-year term elected by the Saeima. President Ulmanis established contacts by visiting world leaders, showing that Latvia was on the road to economic stability. On several occasions he was a guest of President Clinton at the White House. Among his countless accomplishments, President Ulmanis instilled a sense of nationalistic pride.

After serving two terms, President Ulmanis was followed as president by Professor Vaira Vīķe-Feiberga. President Vīķe-Feiberga had left Latvia as a young girl with her parents, fleeing the communist takeover in the early 1940s. She settled in Canada, completed a doctorate in psychology, and became a professor at the University of Montreal. She returned to Latvia in 1998 and won the country's presidency in June 1999. Latvia is now a member of NATO as well as the European Union. President Vīķe-Feiberga has become a dominant force in European

Map 2. Latvia in detail.

politics and has often been compared to Prime Minister Margaret Thatcher. For example, in an article in the *Boston Globe* describing the November 21, 2002, summit in Prague, reporters noted, "But it was President Vaira Vīķe-Feiberga of Latvia—with a moving speech and her dramatic narrative of fleeing her country in World War II, only to return it a half-century later into the Western alliance—who seemed to embody the history in the making at the gathering. 'Our people have been tested in the fires of history, and they have been tempered in the furnaces of suffering and injustice,' Vīķe-Feiberga, 64, said Thursday in her speech. 'They know the meaning and the value of liberty; and they know that it is worth every effort to support it, to maintain it, to stand for it, and to fight for it.' Senior White House officials said President Bush was profoundly moved by her words, and as she spoke without any prepared text before the other 25 heads of state, the room was still and the leaders listened. The U.S. Ambassador to the North Atlantic Treaty Organization, Nicholas Burns, said: 'You could feel what she was saying. There was absolute silence in that room. President Bush was very moved by it, and I believe it was one of the finest speeches I have ever heard in Europe.'"[33] (See appendices 6 and 7 for partial text and press coverage.)

Latvia's social and economic spheres are in an upward spiral, and now that the country has been accepted into NATO and has become a part of the European Union it will flourish even more. Companies from Sweden, Germany, France, Denmark, the United States, and elsewhere around the world have established business ventures in Latvia. With the acceptance of membership in the European community, Latvia's future looks very bright.

On November 21, 2002, NATO invited the Baltic nations and four other countries to join the Atlantic alliance. As President George W. Bush stated in a speech given in Vilnius, Lithuania on November 23, 2002: "The long night of fear, uncertainty and loneliness is over. You're joining the strong and growing family of NATO. Our alliance has made a solemn pledge of protection, and anyone who would choose Lithuania as an enemy has also made an enemy of the United States of America. In the face of aggression, the brave people of Lithuania, Latvia, and Estonia will never again stand alone. . . . You have known cruel oppression and withstood it. You have been held captive by an empire, and you outlived it. And because you have paid its cost, you know the value of human freedom."[34] Now, Latvia is a member of the North Atlantic Treaty Organization (NATO) and the European Union.

The cost has been great both in human suffering and in economic and political oppression. There will be growing pains, but Latvia's growth knows no bounds. Latvia is a shining star, and its future looks very bright indeed.

Fleeing the Homeland: Becoming Human Rubble

In order to understand the Latvian immigrants' success in Michigan, their work ethic and emphasis on education, and that of their children as well, one must look at where they came from and the influences that made them who they are. Also, the effect of these historical nuances have been instilled in first-generation immigrants.

As discussed in the previous chapter, Latvia was in the grip of either German or Russian domination from 1939 to the eventual "serving of the Baltic countries to Stalin" in the early 1940s. In 1939 German forces again took over the Baltic countries. Alexander Cadogan, permanent undersecretary in the British Foreign Office, stated, "It would be useless to protest at the German seizure unless Great Britain was going to fight. . . . If not, than the less said about the district the better."[35] As Mr. Eksteins states, "The Baltic states were the product of happenstance, the unexpected upshot of collapse and confusion. They were not the product of policy but of its ruin. They were nothing to be proud of and as a result not worth defending." The Molotov-Ribbentrop Pact was signed by Germany and Russia in 1939 and essentially gave the Baltic countries to Russia. As Molotov told the Lithuanian foreign minister that small nations had become an anomaly, "Your Lithuania," he said, "along with the other Baltic nations, including Finland, will have to join the glorious family of the Soviet Union."[36] On June 17, 1939, Soviet tanks rolled into Riga. "In the West few noticed. Attention was focused on Hitler's great victory against France as German troops entered Paris."[37] A correspondent of the *Chicago Tribune*, Donald Day, witnessed the arrival of Soviet troops in Riga: "On June 17 there was a mob at the railway station, waving red flags and screaming in hysterical joy about the arrival of the Russians. The Latvian language could not be heard. The speeches, shouts and screams were all in Russian or Yiddish."[38] Rigged elections were held and the elected officials reported to Moscow; the Baltics had become Soviet republics. All semblance of democracy was crushed; rules for churches, schools, publications, radio stations, government agencies, farming, and all facets of life were dictated by the new rulers. Dissidents, Latvian government officials, professionals, and intellectuals were either imprisoned, exiled to work camps in Russia, or shot.

When the Germans returned to Latvia as liberators on July 1, 1941, they were greeted as lost friends.[39] However, the cycle only began again; the Baltic area was to become a protectorate within the greater German Reich, and a puppet government was created. It was apparent that one evil had been replaced by another.

Before the German surrender, Great Britain and the United States showed little or no interest in the plight of the Baltic countries. "Churchill who had been so keen on guaranteeing Baltic independence in 1941, was willing by early 1942 to offer Stalin the Baltic. In March he told Roosevelt 'that the principles of the Atlantic Charter sought not to be construed so as to deny Russia the frontiers she occupied when Germany attacked her.'"[40] Also, Churchill and Roosevelt wanted to shelve territorial issues until a postwar peace treaty could resolve them, "but he [Churchill] doubted that this would be possible in the matter of the Baltic States."[41] Thus Latvia, Lithuania, and Estonia for all practical purposes were looked upon as a Russian frontier, and thus world powers were silent. A vivid example was the way Mr. Peteris Zariņš, the head of the Latvian legation in London, was treated. He wrote a memo asking why nothing was being done with the Soviet takeover of the Baltics and expressing his fear that everyone that did not agree with "the Communist imperialism and their dictatorship will be exterminated by sword and fire; fear and bondage will be again the lot of the Baltic peoples."[42] His official note was not acknowledged; in other words, the Baltic States were no longer acknowledged.[43]

The Yalta Conference

The "Big Three," Roosevelt, Churchill, and Stalin, met in the Crimean resort of Yalta on February 4, 1945. The purpose was to carve out German surrender and the division of Europe. The peoples of Central and Eastern Europe view this conference as a great betrayal. The plight of the Baltic countries was never mentioned. Some historians see the Yalta agreement as a mere "statement of principle," meaning that "the signers have agreed to principles, but that the actual steps will have to be worked out as they begin to cross all the bridges ahead."[44] It is interesting to read the Yalta papers and to find phrases such as "to create democratic institutions of their own choice," "the restoration of sovereign rights and self government," and "our determination to build in cooperation with other peace-loving nations world order under law, dedicated to peace, security, freedom and general well being of all mankind."[45] (See appendix 4 for referenced Yalta papers).

The rest is history: the Baltic nations had lost their independence, a situation that would remain in effect for the next fifty years.

Fleeing the Captors

In the early 1940s Soviet tanks were rolling into Latvia as the Germans were retreating. Many Latvians saw that this was the time to flee their homeland. They had already experienced Soviet occupation once, and had watched as thousands of their compatriots were deported to slave labor camps, were shot in front of their eyes, or simply "disappeared," never to be heard from again. People gathered what they could carry and left with the retreating German soldiers. A gentleman I interviewed recounted his memories of leaving Latvia. Together with his two brothers and parents, he had packed a suitcase and taken a train to Kurzeme to his grandparents' farm. There, together with their grandparents, they sat in three wagons pulled by horses and traveled to Liepāja, which is a port city on the Baltic Sea. By some miracle they were able to board a

German cargo ship and eventually landed in Germany. Here they boarded a train and traveled to the mountains of Czechoslovakia. His father had obtained a position with the Czech government, patrolling forests to prevent illegal chopping of wood. This was in exchange for living quarters and some food. Everyone who escaped Latvia at that time had similar stories to tell; they took what they could carry and fled to either Sweden by boat or to Germany. When the family heard that the war had ended, they decided to seek refuge in Germany. They resided in a variety of displaced persons' camps and eventually settled in the Wurzburg Central Camp (Wurzburgas Centrālā Nometne).

An older gentleman recounted an experience he had during these desperate times. He had three young boys, a pregnant wife, and his parents to provide for and starvation was imminent. They had been walking on foot, seeking refuge in southeastern Germany. One night he crept into a farmer's potato patch and stole a bag of potatoes so his family would not die of starvation. They could not boil the potatoes because the fire would be seen; thus for four days they subsided on the uncooked vegetables. He said that he was an honest man, and often wished that he could return, find the farmer, and repay him for his loss. Yet Germany and most of Western Europe was filled with starving, disoriented people who had lost their homeland and had no place to seek refuge.

In the chaos at the end of the World War II many saw the refugees as an undesirable element. "Like the debris in the streets, the authorities wanted to get rid of this 'human rubble' as quickly as possible."[46] One British official even called them "'the scum of Europe.'"[47]

Before America had entered the war it was plain to everyone that the devastation, poverty, and suffering resulting from the conflict would be so great that an agency would need to be developed to deal with the problems. On November 9, 1943, the representatives of the forty-four member countries of the United Nations met at the White House and signed an agreement.[48] This was the formation of the United Nations Relief and Rehabilitation Administration (hereafter referred to as UNRRA), whose purpose was to offer humanitarian aid to the multitude of homeless people then roaming Western Europe. Officially there was a formula for how member countries would

Bombs and Beethoven

While the Latvians were fleeing their land, many experienced the bombings and desecration caused by war. As Modris Eksteins writes in his book *Walking Since Daybreak:* "A bomb had landed on the next street. Our building, while still standing, had been badly damaged. The windows were all gone, the walls unstable. The jar of honey my mother had battle to acquire the day before for her sick daughter lay shattered on the floor. A flower she had found, in the midst of winter, and put in a vase on the windowsill lay crushed among the ruins. 'I often ask myself,' wrote Mathilde Wolff-Monckeberg, 'what this period of time will look like in our memory. Which particular picture will demand precedence over the others, and will there ever be a time without screeching sirens, without above us the deafening crashes of explosions, and within us fear and worry? . . . Whenever I listen to Beethoven, I cry'" (200).

contribute to this effort, but the financial burden eventually came to rest almost entirely on the United States (72%) and Great Britain (13%).[49] The hope was that many refugees would be repatriated; when conditions settled down, people from these lands would be expected to return to their homelands. However, very few Balts wanted to return to their homelands after the war, and they were generally regarded as nonrepatriable.[50] An estimate is that about 1,576 Latvians decided to return to their homeland.[51]

Thus, Latvian immigrants sought shelter in the many camps. These "camps" in the beginning took many forms. Some were makeshift tent cities, old prison camps, or army buildings. Some immigrants were placed in private homes, hotels, or pensions. In the beginning, the organizers placed many nationalities in one camp, but they soon saw that this did not work and began to segregate the immigrants from different countries into individual facilities. In 1945 several Latvian organizations were founded with support from UNRRA. These included "Latviešu Centrālā Komiteja" (LCK), "Latvijas Centrālā Padome" (LCP), and "Latvijas Nacionālā Padome" (LNP).[52] The purpose of these organizations was to unify all the Latvian immigrants, to

A Misconception of Displaced Persons

Many people did not see the displaced persons as people in need, especially many local Germans, who berated and despised them: "The DP's the 'foreigners,' were insufferable. They swarmed like Patton's locusts over all available housing; they snatched like rats anything resembling food; and, given half a chance, they would carry away anything that wasn't nailed down. They stole money and ration coupons from the elderly; they beat up innocent citizens for fun; they slaughtered farm animals in the dark of night and spirited the carcasses away; they engaged in firefights with the police; they lived like monstrous beasts, filthy and licentious. In the transit camps in winter anything made of wood–beds, tables, window frames, even floorboards–was burned. And so it went. Incident after incident. Such was the popular image of the DP's" (Eksteins, *Walking Since Daybreak*, 119). Such animosity is understandable. Germany had been desecrated by the war. The Germans were broken, disillusioned, starving and many were homeless. To add to their misery, thousands of people were now swarming to their country using up needed resources and often taking existing jobs.

find suitable housing for the immigrants, and to help each camp organize. Germany was divided into four zones: British, U.S., French, and Soviet. Latvians found refuge in several camps, including Augsburgas Camp, which housed about 2,200 Latvians[53]; Fisbahas Camp, with about 1,500; Hanavas Camp near Frankfurt, which housed about 1,000; Manheimas Camp, which housed 1,100; Bloomberg Camp, which housed 1,500; Flensburg Camp, which housed 1,500; Libeka Camp, which housed 6,000; and Valka Camp and Wurzburg Camp, which together housed 525 Latvians in two camp areas.[54]

Many local Germans were jealous of the way the Latvians were organizing their camps and receiving aid from UNRRA. The Baltic people were used to a higher standard of living, and that their goal was to create a livable and organized habitat.[55] Also, military officials and UNRRA workers were inclined to give the maximum self-government to each camp and nationality. The Baltic camps had some of the best administrative talent. "In fact, most of the former officials of the Baltic governments were located right there in the D.P. camps."[56]

The Latvian camps each had a director and a number of other administrators. A microcosm of society was established in each. Medical and dental facilities were established using their own nurses, dentists, and physicians. Schools were immediately established; there was an abundance of former teachers at all levels. Ministers held church services, self-governing legal entities were founded, and all forms of cultural activities blossomed. For example, most Latvian camps had their own choir, artists who exhibited their works, writers, and theater troupes who performed plays. Some films were even made. Also, newsreels were produced, ballet performances were held, folk dancing was taught and performed by various age groups, newspapers and books were published, and various sports leagues were founded. The Latvian tradition is ingrained with song and dance, and song festivals were held where choirs from several camps would perform, followed by evening festivities. In other words, the Latvians did not sit around waiting for others to organize and create their society; they did it on their own. Moreover, those who were not active in the camp functions could often find work in the local German towns.[57]

Finding Sponsors: Looking toward the Future

UNRRA was viewed as a "short-term" organization, because it did not cover the long-term problem of the nonrepatriable displaced persons, and it had not been established to carry out resettlement. Furthermore, it was not authorized under its Articles of Agreement to deal with those people who refused to return to their homelands, and many of the grants that funded the organization expired in 1947.[58] Thus, the International Refugee Organization (hereafter referred to as IRO) was established. This organization functioned more or less as an enormous employment agency, every month receiving quotas from different countries who would accept the displaced persons. It is interesting to note that 40 percent of the available visas would go to former residents of the Baltic States and people from eastern Poland.[59] Hence, under the wings of the IRO, relief agencies in the United States offered to sponsor

Latvian families leaving a displaced persons camp for America, 1949. Photo provided by S. Meija.

families and locate jobs and housing for them. There were many agencies that worked at the grass roots level; most often they were religious groups such as Catholic, Baptist, and Lutheran congregations throughout the United States.

Thus, this brings us to how Latvians found work in and immigrated to Michigan.

Finding New Homes in Michigan

Kalamazoo

People have often wondered why Kalamazoo has been such an active Latvian enclave. The first Latvian immigration to the area can be pinpointed to the late 1940s and began with the help of Jānis Laupmanis. Mr. Laupmanis emigrated from Latvia around 1937, married a local woman, and became a Methodist minister, establishing a small congregation on East Main Street.[60] In 1948, Mr. E. Dīnvalds, his wife Milda and sons Raimonds and Valfrids and his family left the displaced persons' camp ("Valka," in Germany) and settled in Kalamazoo. Mr. Dīnvalds had been working for UNRRA and IRO at the Valka camp and was fluent in English.[61] By chance he met and befriended Rev. Laupmanis. Both knew that there were countless Latvian families still in the camps in need of sponsors. During this time, Mr. Ernest Brože was the secretary for the Valkas governing committee. His friend Mr. Dīnvalds had already settled in Kalamazoo, and both men had a vision: they wished to bring the whole Latvian choir, "Shield of Songs" (Dziesmu Vairogs), to Michigan, with the help of Rev. Laupmanis. As mentioned previously, folk music was ingrained in the Latvian culture, and this particular choir had been founded at the Valka camp. The choir had gained an outstanding reputation for its performances.[62] Rev. **27**

Laupmanis called a meeting of some sixty Kalamazoo pastors, seeking placement for the known Latvian choir members in Valka; he found that the local congregations were supportive and enthusiastic and wanted to sponsor some one hundred choir members and their families.[63] Mr. Dīnvalds, having received an enthusiastic reply from Rev. Laupmanis, wrote to Ernests Brože at the Valka camp, requesting to sponsor a number of families.[64] At this time Mr. Arnolds Kalnājs and his family had the opportunity to obtain a sponsor in the Kalamazoo area.[65] Mr. Kalnājs was a composer in addition to being the director for the Valkas camp choir. Correspondence ensued between Rev. Laupmanis and Mr. Brože, which resulted in the former promising and providing sponsors for the majority of the choir members.[66] As Rev. Laupmanis stated, "one of my goals is to use the choir and short speeches as a tool to fight communism and awaken the American people from a deep sleep, so that they may see the tricks communists play."[67] As Mr. Ojars Brūveris writes in his autobiography, "Yes, Rev. Laupmanis, Dīnvalds and Brože were truly angels from heaven with a devotion to their Latvian heritage, perhaps unsurpassed by anyone. It was their combined effort and work that brought over more than one hundred choir members and their families plus many others as their relatives and friends learned of the three angels and knocked on their hearts pleading for help. And they helped."[68]

The members of the choir were concerned that if they accepted Rev. Laupmanis's invitation, they would have to join the Methodist church. Rev. Laupmanis responded by saying that "it does not mean that you must join my church nor change your faith. Matters of the soul are sacred and personal; only God and each individual has the right to change their faith."[69]

By the early 1950s many choir members had already found sponsors in the area and had found gainful employment, and choir practices were being held. On Sundays, the choir members would meet at the Methodist church before the service and practice. During the church service the choir would sing a few songs. Afterward, Rev. Laupmanis, together with the choir, would travel to outlying churches. He would hold a church service, incorporating lectures on the evils of communism, and would inspire the listeners with the Latvian songs. Often,

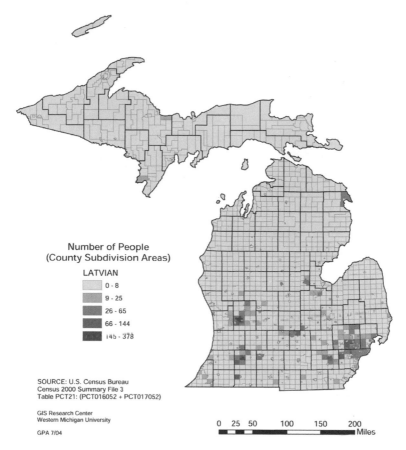

Number of People
(County Subdivision Areas)

LATVIAN

0 - 8
9 - 25
26 - 65
66 - 144
145 - 378

SOURCE: U.S. Census Bureau
Census 2000 Summary File 3
Table PCT21: (PCT016052 + PCT017052)

GIS Research Center
Western Michigan University

GPA 7/04

0   25   50   100   150   200
Miles

Map 3. Distribution of Michgan's population claiming Latvian ancestry, 2004.

they would visit two churches on a given Sunday, not returning home until after midnight.[70] In addition to their political goal, these presentations had another goal as well—to find additional sponsors and to bring more Latvians from the displaced persons' camps to settle in the area. A law had been passed that immigrants were to work for the sponsor for eighteen months; only after this period had elapsed could they seek different employment.[71] Slowly, most of the choir members found sponsors. Family members, fraternity brothers, friends, and neighbors were sponsored by those who had already relocated to the area. Immigration to the Kalamazoo area was not limited only to persons from the "Valka" displaced persons camp, but included Latvians from a variety of camps. Thus the colony began to grow and by the mid-1950s more than two thousand had settled in Kalamazoo.[72]

In July 1949, I arrived in America as a two-month-old, with my parents, three brothers, and grandparents. Because I was a newborn, we had gotten transportation from Germany to Boston on an old army transport plane. Our intermediate sponsor was in New Hampshire, where the first winter my father worked for a farmer, clearing a forest for grazing land and earning twenty-five cents an hour. Corresponding with friends who had been in the same camp in Germany, my parents found that many Latvians had settled in the Kalamazoo area. We were fortunate to find a man who owned a large fruit farm outside of Coloma, Michigan. In the spring of 1950, a neighboring farmer offered to drive our family in his open pickup to the nearest train station, where we boarded a train bound for the Midwest. Two days later we arrived in Niles, Michigan. The Coloma farmer sponsored several families and provided living quarters in small houses scattered in nearby locations. If one is familiar with *Grapes of Wrath* by John Steinbeck, an accurate pictorial image could be garnered. We were immigrants, poverty-stricken, owning only what we could carry in small suitcases, and the majority not even knowing the language of our new, adopted land. Yet, there was a difference between these new immigrants and the people described in Steinbeck's novel, because most Latvian immigrants had an education and had worked in their professions for many years in their home country. They had owned apartments in Riga, and were socially and culturally astute. Also, many of those arriving in Michigan had had their own prosperous farms and had extensive knowledge of agrarian practices. We were coming to a new country with very little in our pockets but we had the American dream in mind; we knew life could and would be better. The key was freedom and opportunity.

More than a dozen Latvian families lived and worked on farms in the Coloma area. The men and women worked in the fields during the day. The school-aged children attended the local country school. The grandmothers cared for the newborns and toddlers. The older men repaired the farm equipment, and everyone worked in their individual gardens. My father earned fifty-five cents per hour, and mother made forty-five cents. Since my father did not have a driver's license, he tilled the soil with a horse and plow. During the harvest season everyone, regardless of age, worked to pick the fruit, and all were paid by the flat.

Our lives were much easier than those of many, for we were given a four-room house, and though it had no indoor plumbing or heat, it did have electricity. The wooden stove in the kitchen served for cooking as well as heat. The kind farmer presented our family with a cow that gave milk, and my grandmother could make butter. On Friday evenings, the farmer loaned all the workers a pickup truck. Fruit crates were placed in the center of the flat bed and covered with blankets. Everyone would pile in and sit on the makeshift seats in great anticipation of the trip to town. It was not an idyllic, bucolic existence, but one of grueling hard work and poverty; yet there was the dream of a better life in the future.

My mother and aunt were some of the lucky ones, for they had gotten additional employment; during the night, they would clean offices in the local town. In their "spare time" they sewed curtains for a small, local company. Eventually my mother found work as an assistant for a local dentist who was surprised that she had had a thriving dental practice in Latvia for a number of years. This account is not extreme, but the norm. Every Latvian family who came to America went through this same process; only the surroundings were minutely different. Some found work in factories in large urban areas. Many families found employment picking cotton or tobacco in southern states. There are countless such stories.

The families in the Coloma area knew that many Latvians from the displaced persons camps had immigrated to Kalamazoo. The goal was to have contact with other Latvians in Kalamazoo and begin social interactions. My father often said that his employer was not pleased with this endeavor. He feared that we would see that life was better in the city; men would be working for better wages at the Eckrich sausage factory, at the paper mills, at the Shakespeare Company making fishing tackle, at the Gibson guitar company, at the local hospitals, and so on. Eventually, he feared, one by one he would lose his hard workers. This eventually did happen. It was a big day when our family purchased a black 1939 Chevy and could now make the three-hour journey to Kalamazoo to attend church, choir practice, and various other social events. One by one, we all left the Coloma farm, moving to either neighboring towns or the city of Kalamazoo.

These were the seeds of the Latvian community in Kalamazoo. Families sponsored friends and relatives. Everyone arrived with little or nothing; no money, food, or place to live. Families who had already established themselves helped others. For example, Ernests and Olga Brože had already purchased a house not far from West Main Avenue. This was an almost unheard of feat because only a few families were able to do this. They opened their door to newly arriving families. Often there were more than ten people living in the small home.

Thus, Latvians began to flock to the Kalamazoo area and to establish organizations. On June 30, 1950, the Kalamazoo Latvian Association (Kalamazū Latviešu Biedrība) was established.[73] Meetings and larger social events were held at Rev. Laupmanis's church hall or at the YMCA or YWCA.[74] In 1955 the association purchased a hall in the Oakwood area in which to hold social events.[75] The building was renovated by its members; the men spent almost every evening and weekend reconstructing the building. They would come home from work, eat dinner, change clothes, and work until midnight. Those men who had night shifts in the paper mills spent their days in rebuilding. The upstairs had a smaller hall where local artists would exhibit their works, meetings would be held, or the literary guild would offer readings. The folk dancing practices were also held here, as well as the ladies craft auxiliary meetings, and weekly choir practices and other events. The larger hall in the walk-out basement was intended for the frequent larger social gatherings.

Under the umbrella of this organization, various activities blossomed. The most prominent was the establishment of the Latvian school in 1952.[76] The school was headed by a principal and guided by a board comprised of parents. Also, a school library was established in 1957, containing approximately three thousand books in the beginning.[77] Classes were held on Saturday mornings at a local school, and later the Latvian school was moved to the Latvian church hall on Rose Street.

The Lutheran congregations were a focal point of the community. On December 10, 1949, Reverend Jānis Turks held the first church service for the community.[78] That same year the Saint John's Latvian

A young girl in a traditional folk costume.
Photo by S. Meija.

Lutheran Church was founded with five hundred members.[79] Services were held at local, rented churches until 1961, when the first Latvian-owned church in the United States was built on Cherryhill Drive. Also in 1950 the Kalamazoo Latvian Church was founded with Rev. A. Piebalgs as the minister. This congregation also had about five hundred parishioners, and they purchased a church on Portage Street in 1965.[80] The two congregations unified in 1994 and continue to be active today as a single unit. In 1952 a chapter of the "Daugavas Vanagi" was established with approximately 150 members and it continues to be active today. In 1956 the Girl Scout and Boy Scout Kalamazoo chapter was founded; also a sports division, student club, fraternity and sorority council, and youth group were established.[81] In 1964 a chapter of the Latvian Credit Union was established. Most Latvians in Michigan by this time had established themselves by finding gainful employment and purchasing homes. They were becoming part of the local community, yet establishing their own cultural and ethnic activities filled the need to continue and pass on their rich heritage.

No discussion of Kalamazoo would be complete without examining the establishment of the Latvian Student Center, which was affiliated with Western Michigan University, and the Latvian language classes, which were part of the Department of Linguistics and the Division of Continuing Education. The quest to maintain the Latvian language was essential, especially with the "russification" of people in Latvia, and thus in 1966-67 Dr. Valdis Muižnieks, a well-known local chiropractor, began weekend Latvian language courses for young adults.[82] In 1968 a summer semester program was developed, and in the fall semester of 1981 Dr. L. Muižniece was hired as assistant professor to create the opportunity for sixteen students to obtain a minor in Latvian. In 1983 the reorganized Department of Language and Linguistics gave students the opportunity to also obtain a major in the language. Classes included in this course of study were an introduction to Latvian and a variety of courses covering composition, literature, life and culture, the methodology of teaching Latvian, Latvian history, and so on.[83] Between 1966 and 1980 around 650 students from various parts of the United States and five foreign countries attended the program. The program flourished because of the enthusiastic support of Dr. Robert Palmatier and Dr. Bruce Clarke, as well as the American Latvian Association in Washington, D.C. This program was the only one of its kind, outside of Latvia, where students could obtain both a major and minor in the Latvian language. By 1994, when the program was phased out due to lack of funds, it had had over one thousand participants.[84] In January 1982 the Student Center (Jāņa Riekstiņa Studiju Centris) was completed and those students attending Western's Latvian program had a dormitory and Lithuanian and Estonian students could also utilize the facility.[85] The structure was funded by private donations, from the American Latvian Association as well as other organizations.[86] Eventually it housed an extensive library containing books, microfilm, recordings, maps, and videos, as well as art objects.[87] Again, because of a lack of funds to maintain the endeavor, the American Latvian Association sold the building in 1996.[88]

In 1985 Rev. J. Turks initiated the purchase of a parcel of land next to the Latvian church to build a new hall to fill the expanding social needs of the community. The Latvian Center (Latviešu Centris) was completed in 1987 and still functions today as the focal point of the community, housing both the Kalamazoo Latvian Association and the Latvian School.[89]

The Kalamazoo Latvian community has formed a variety of choirs, ensembles, and singing groups, some of which are still active today. Almost from the founding of the community there have been folk dancing groups, literary and journalistic groups, music publications and artist groups, and many other organizations. From 1976 to 1996 the Western Michigan University radio station had regular weekly programs called "The Sound of Latvian Music."[90] The majority of the community's deceased members are buried in Riverside Cemetery. In late fall a memorial service is held where candles are lit on each grave; in the summer there is another similar memorial service.

Today, much of the community's organizational leadership has been taken over by the first and second generations. Many are active in the previously listed organizations but have also carved out successful lives in the greater Kalamazoo area. Individuals of Latvian heritage work as policemen and firemen, and as psychologists, dentists, physicians, and attorneys. In addition, several own successful businesses. Many Latvians work for Western Michigan University, as faculty, administrators, or support staff. They are not active only in Latvian organizations but also as participants in their children's school activities, and in social and humanitarian agencies. No matter what field they have entered or what job they possess, Latvians are held in high regard and have a reputation for being hardworking, educated, honest, and an asset to their communities.

Detroit

The Latvian community in Detroit has an interesting history. The first known Latvians came to the area after the 1905 revolution in Russia. Later immigrants joined them after the 1917 Revolution and World War II.[91] Most of these people still held on to their old political and sociological ideologies; some even declared that it was a grave mistake to separate from the "Mother Country Russia." They felt that a free Latvia had always been a mistake and they were pleased that this had been rectified with the communist occupation in 1940-41 and 1944-45.[92] These first Latvian immigrants are often referred to as "Old Latvians" (Veclatvieši), and their ideological thoughts never left the czarist "mentality." They could not comprehend accounts that Latvia had declared independence in 1918 and had become a flourishing, economically thriving, and democratic country. They failed to see how the omnipotent "Mother Russia" had plundered Latvia, stifling its socioeconomic development and depriving the country of freedom and democracy.[93]

These "old Latvians" founded an association (Latviešu Biedrība) and purchased a hall to hold meetings and various social events on Lahser Avenue. They felt that keeping their heritage, culture, and language alive was not essential. Most of the second generation did not speak the language or participate in cultural events. The association's members dwindled yearly, and by the end of 1949 there were only about seventeen participants.[94]

One of the first immigrants to the Detroit area, around 1949, was Ludmila Ritiņa. She met and married Augusts Jēkabsons, who was a descendent from one of the "old Latvian" families. Mr. Jēkabsons was born in the United States, but had traveled with his parents to Latvia and had attended school there for a period of time.[95] His ideas about the perpetuation of the Latvian culture, language, and heritage were in sharp contrast to those of his predecessors; thus he greatly supported his new wife's quest to help relocate Latvian displaced persons who still lived in Germany. Mrs. Jēkabsons befriended Reverend Harry Wolf, who was the director of Lutheran Charities of Detroit. They spent countless hours at social events and talked to anyone who would listen about the wretched plight of the Communist takeover of Latvia and how they had been forced to flee their homeland with only what they could carry. Mrs. Jēkabsons described the poverty and disheartment people faced in displaced persons' camps, not knowing where they would be transferred, where they would make their new homes, and how they would make a living. The goal was to obtain sponsors from organizations and individuals in the Detroit area and this eventually began the slow influx of immigration. It should be noted that Anna and Krists Jēkabsons, Augusts's parents, were also instrumental in this undertaking.[96]

The pursuit of nationalism and cultural preservation began with the arrival of Mr. Sigurds Rudzītis and his family as well as Mr. Dainis Rudzītis and his family. Together with several other families, their thought was to establish and unify the existing and newly arriving Latvians.[97] There was a plan to join the existing Latvian Association, but the newly arrived immigrants' ideologies did not mesh with the existing group's philosophies. Those who were now coming to this country had seen and lived in a free Latvia and were filled with national pride. They had lived through and seen the horrors of the Communist and German occupations and had fled their homeland to be cloistered in camps, not knowing what their future would bring.[98] On February 28, 1950, a meeting was held in which the "old Latvian" contingency submitted a plan and guidelines for revitalizing the existing Latvian Association. The new immigrants refused to accept the plan and the old guard left. This was the beginning of a new organization called the "Latvian Association of Detroit" (LAD/Latviešu Apvienība Detroitā).[99] Not only did this organization take the reins in guiding the community in cultural and social events but it was also instrumental in the struggle in the national-political arena to gain independence for Latvia.[100]

As sponsors were located and immigrants arrived from the displaced persons' camps, most joined the newly established Latvian Association of Detroit. Some of the newcomers attended Rev. Wolf's church services, but it was apparent that there was a need to establish a Latvian church. Saint Paul's Latvian Lutheran Church (Sv. Pauļa Eveņģēliskā Luterāņu Draudze) was founded on May 21, 1950. The Rev. Jānís Turks traveled from Kalamazoo to hold the first church service.[101] It should be noted that Rev. Turks gave his utmost in the founding of congregations throughout Michigan and the propagation of the Christian faith. He worked full time in a factory supporting his wife and three children. In the evenings and on the weekends he served as minister for the St. John's congregation in Kalamazoo. Also, every Sunday, after the regular service in his own church, together with Mr. Valters Grīnbergs, the organist, he would drive to Detroit, Lansing, St. Joseph, and other

A group of Detroit Latvian school students, 1985. Photo provided by U. Grinbergs.

cities to hold services. He would officiate at funerals, weddings, chris-
tenings, and confirmations when needed.

On October 14, 1951, the Latvian Catholic Group was founded. In
May 1952 the Christ's Church (Kristus Draudze) congregation was
founded. This congregation had the benefit of receiving a bequest of a
hotel located in Pontiac, Michigan. This helped ensure economic stability for the congregation and later supported the purchase of the
Latvian Center "Garezers" and surrounding land parcels for the development of a community of homes (Latviešu ciems).[102] The two congregations have now unified.

In September 1950 the Latvian School was founded under the guidance of LAD (Latvian Association Detroit), and in 1986 it became an
independent organization.[103] There have been more than sixty students
at times, and classes have been held at various locations over the years.
Presently, classes are held at the LAD center, which is housed in the St.
Paul's Church social hall. Parents and individuals who enjoy working
with children staff the elementary school, as in all Latvian communities in Michigan. The children are taught the language, both reading
and writing, history, geography, and religion. They have a school choir
as well as instruction in folk dancing. Parents bring their children from
Ann Arbor, Toledo, and other outlying areas.

Both Girl Scout and Boy Scout activities have been extremely pop-ular in the Latvian community since the early 1950s. Mr. Fricis Sīpols was instrumental in establishing the movement in Detroit and has worked actively within the movement ever since. The troops follow the Latvian scouting guidelines, which have been developed to fit the American scouting standards. All instruction is done in Latvian, and the Boy Scouts and Girl Scouts participate in annual camping trips with troops from other Latvian communities.

In 1963 the Latvian Credit Union was established under the spon-sorship of the St. Paul's Church.[104] It is still active today and follows all state and federal mandated guidelines.

The Detroit Latvian community has been extremely active on the political front since the mid-1950s. One must remember that Latvia was lost to the Communists just prior to this time, and the majority of Latvian immigrants came to this area seeking political asylum. The Detroit area has many ethnic groups, including Poles, Germans, Italians, Greeks, Ukrainians, and Lithuanians. Representatives from

Latvian Association in Detroit president D. Rudzitis, Southwest Captive Nations President P. Austrins, M. Sints, Governor W. Milliken, Detroit Captive Nations President S. Rudzitis, R. Kempe, L. Jekabsons, and J. Pavasars, 1969. Photo pro-vided by D. Rudzitis.

The New Latvian Americans

The Latvian culture and tradition is still being instilled in younger generations of Latvian Americans. A good example can be seen with Diana Sydlowski, who lives in the Detroit area with her husband and their infant daughter.

Both sets of Diana's grandparents came to America via the displaced persons camps in Germany. Each family had several small children. Her mother, Marite (Runka) Grinbergs, grew up in Milwaukee, Wisconsin. Marite was immersed in the local Latvian society, participating in youth groups, church activities, and the Latvian sports club. Diana's father, Ugis Grinbergs, grew up in Kalamazoo, Michigan. He too participated in all of the Latvian cultural undertakings: school, church, scouts, youth group and sports club. Marite and Ugis met at a Latvian Sports festival in Milwaukee. After marriage, Diana's parents settled in the Detroit area and Diana and her two younger sisters were brought up in two cultures. They attended the local public schools and were extremely active socially and especially in athletics. However, at home the family spoke only Latvian, and they regularly attended the Latvian-speaking activities of weekend school, girl scouts, church, sports activities, and other Latvian associations. Diana's mother took active part as a Girl Scout leader, church ladies auxiliary member, and sports club member. Ugis was active as scoutmaster of a Latvian troop, sports club manager, member of several Latvian associations,

these various ethnic groups came together to form the Captive Nations Committee. The purpose of this committee was to inform Michigan residents of the evils of communism and of how homelands had been forcefully taken away. In 1959 President Eisenhower, in a proclamation, established an annual Captive Nations Week. This week was commemorated with parades, proclamations, press releases, and an audience with the mayor and governor. In 1959, due to lobbying from the Captive Nations Committee, the mayor of Detroit and Governor Williams refused to meet with Nikita Krushchev's deputy, who had expressed an interest to visiting Detroit.[105] In 1957 the Latvians joined the newly formed Baltic Committee. One of this organization's accomplishments was to lobby in 1966 for the expansion of the Voice of America, which and especially with the Latvian church, as a twenty-three-year member of the board of directors, of which he has served as council president and board chairman for thirteen years. These activities were important to assuring continuance of the Latvian Lutheran faith, culture, and ethnic values.

Diana's parents came to the United States as very small children, but their parents instilled within them the Latvian language and traditions. Diana is first-generation American, but also was raised to know the Latvian language, culture, traditions, and heritage. In the spring of 1999 she married Michael Sydlowski, who is of Polish descent. They now have an infant daughter with the Latvian name of Kaija Emma. Michael is slowly learning Latvian and totally supports raising his daughter in his wife's footsteps—familiar with and active in two cultures. The young couple has decided to speak Latvian with their daughter, and to take her to Latvian school, church, summer camp, sport clubs, and other Latvian activities.

The Sydlowski family is an example of second-generation Latvian Americans preserving the language, culture, and heritage of their ancestry. They plan to instill these beliefs and traditions in their children, hoping that they, in turn, will pass them on to the next generation. In order for the Latvian culture and traditions to survive, it is necessary for other young couples with Latvian heritage to support and embrace the same quest.

would produce cultural programs and offer news to nations behind the iron curtain.[106] The Latvian Association of Detroit (LAD) has also been active in the International Institute, where in annual festivals they organize booths to offer traditional foods, exhibit various artistic endeavors, and disseminate information about Latvia.

There are countless Latvian-Americans in the Detroit area who have worked effortlessly to establish and preserve the Latvian cultural heritage and traditions. The Latvians have integrated themselves into all aspects of the Detroit community and have made many contributions. Many individuals work either for the auto industry or in businesses that are associated with the industry (the majority being engineers). In addition, within the community there are doctors, den-

*Detroit Latvian fraternity and sorority sponsored Kalpaka balle, 2001. Photo pro-
vided by Mr. and Mrs. A. Broze.*

tists, teachers and professors, builders, business owners, attorneys, a
catering company, and a number working in city government.[107] In
addition, there are a few who have achieved worldwide recognition. For
example, Mr. Gunnar Birkerts, an American with Latvian roots, was a
professor of architecture at the University of Michigan from 1959 to
1990. He has designed countless impressive structures, including the
Museum of Glass in Corning, New York; the Federal Reserve Bank of
Minneapolis, Minnesota; the addition to the University of Michigan
Law Library; the United States Embassy in Caracas, Venezuela; the
Church of the Servant in Kentwood, Michigan; and the Cross of Christ
Church in Bloomfield Hills, Michigan.[108] His designs and structures
have received worldwide acclaim.[109] His son, Sven Birkerts, who was
raised in the Detroit area, is very accomplished in the literary field. He
is a faculty member at Mount Holyoke and Bennington Colleges and
has published countless essays, monographs, and books. He has
received undivided praise for his most recent book, *My Sky Blue Trades:
Growing up Counter in a Contrary Time.*[110]

     Dr. Juris Upatnieks, a professor at the University of Michigan, is one
of two scientists who have made tremendous contributions to today's
modern holography equipment. He and his colleagues theorized that
holography could be used as a three-dimensional visual presentation.

Drs. Leith and Upatnieks happened upon previous work on holography by Dr. Dennis Gabor, a 1971 Nobel Prize winner, and decided to apply this theory with newly invented laser light sources. The result was the first laser transmission hologram of a 3-D object.[111]

In the early days of Latvian immigration, Mrs. Astra Kalniņš was very active in the establishment of opera in the community and sang with the Detroit City Opera.[112] Mrs. Mirdza Leimanis established a dance studio and gave private lessons to local residents, some of whom went on to dance in the American Ballet in New York as well as on Broadway.[113] Because of her artistic ability and her professional accomplishments, she was invited to join the Scabbard Club, which is an exclusive organization for artists who have achieved acclaim in their fields.[114]

Grand Rapids

Grand Rapids is another major Latvian community in Michigan. Many of the first immigrants to the area were members of the choir from the Valka camp in Germany (Shield of Song, "Dziesmu Vairogs").[115] At the time Richard M. Bressler was head of a local aid agency, the "Aid to Displaced Persons Corporation," which helped find sponsors for the immigrants.[116] In 1949 the Latvians already settled in the community created a committee to assist Mr. Bressler in bringing more settlers from the displaced persons' camps in Germany, but the committee ended its work in 1952 because immigration to the area had all but ceased.[117] Between 1949 and 1952 there were approximately 1,000 Latvians who had settled in the Grand Rapids area.[118]

On April 7, 1951, the Grand Rapids Latvian Association was founded.[119] The organization's goal was to support any endeavor that would aid in gaining Latvian independence.[120] The new Latvian immigrants used every opportunity to show their community the injustice of the Soviet occupation of Latvia and the unspeakable horrors that had been bestowed upon their countrymen. They organized demonstrations and wrote letters to the president and members of Congress.[121] The founders' mission was also to support the Latvian youth in their pursuit to obtain a higher education while still maintaining their own language and culture. The thought was that the young people who maintained their cultural identity would be among those who would return to a free Latvia to establish a new democracy.[122] In 1951 the association decided to purchase a center at 340/342 Bridge Street. All members worked diligently to remodel the three-story structure so that it would be conducive to meetings, concerts, theater productions, and large social gatherings.[123] Because of the construction of US-131 the building was sold and a new facility was built and opened on October 19, 1963. A local Latvian architect, A. Linde, designed the plans, and a Latvian builder, V. Ostrovs, built it. Most members of the association worked countless hours helping with the construction; over 319 persons worked more than 6,626 hours without compensation.

Under the wing of the Latvian Association there were many groups and organizations that unified the community. There were writers and a literary society, a very popular theater group, folk dancing groups, Boy Scouts and Girl Scouts, a credit union, various choirs and sports leagues, a youth group, and a club for retirees. Also, as in the Kalamazoo and Detroit communities, a school for children was founded almost from the beginning. The Latvians worked hard not only to establish their own cultural pursuits but also to educate themselves and their children and find lucrative employment in the Grand Rapids area.

Around 1951, Catholic Bishop Jazeps Rancans, who had been a member of the Latvian parliament, immigrated to this area. He also used every opportunity to expound to the local community about Latvian occupation and the ill effects of communism.[124] In 1954 the first Latvian Catholic church in Grand Rapids was purchased on Mt. Vernon Street. Because the land was needed by the state, however, a new church was purchased and the first mass was read on May 20, 1961.[125] The Catholic congregation is still active today but a local pastor conducts services; the liturgy is read in English by the pastor and the congregation responds in Latvian.

The first Lutheran church in the community was founded in 1949 and by the early 1950s there were two congregations with over a thousand members combined. Over the years there have been five ministers who have served the Latvian community, the present one having emigrated from Latvia in 1999 to take over the now unified congregation.

The Grand Rapids Lutheran Congregation with the Latvian Archbishop E. Rozitis. (Front row) A. Ruperts, Rev. I. Goforth, The Archbishop, Rev. U. Cepure, (second row) Rev. D. Skudrina, Rev. L. Zusevics, (back row) Rev. L. Viksna, Rev. G. Lazdins, Rev. G. Puidza, Rev. J. Mednis, and Rev. G. Silars. Photo by A. Ruperts.

The congregation now has approximately 226 members and has a beautiful church located at 1780 Knapp Street NE.[126]

The Latvians in Grand Rapids have always been active politically. They not only organized Captive Nations meetings, parades, and demonstrations, but were frequently visited by local and national political leaders. For example, President Gerald Ford frequently visited and spoke at various functions in the community, and the folk dancing group "Liesma" was invited to perform in Washington, D.C., in 1972.

Today, there are four active organizations in the Grand Rapids Latvian community: the Latvian Association, the Grand Rapids Evangelical Lutheran Church, the Catholic congregation, and the "Daugavas Vanagi." Because of lack of participants, the Latvian School was disbanded, but parents still take their young children to the school in Kalamazoo.

In 1963 the Grand Rapids Latvian Lutheran church purchased an approximately eighty-acre parcel of land south of the city; about ten

The Grand Rapids Latvian Folk dancing group Liesma with Vice-president Gerald Ford in front of the Capitol Building, Washington, D.C., 1972. Photo provided by O. Jansons.

miles north of Allegan in Allegan county. The area is called "Mežvidi" (Middle of the Woods) and its purpose is to provide a place for Sunday gatherings for the congregation from May to September, to celebrate Saint John's Day, and to hold family gatherings and celebrations such as weddings, confirmations, and other functions. Also, the first children's summer camp was held there in 1963. The area has one large community building with a kitchen and four sleeping cabins accommodating ten to fifteen people.[127] When visiting these idyllic, bucolic surroundings, Walden Pond comes to mind! Today the land is rented out to other churches, organizations and scout troops.

Latvians have become an integral part of the larger Grand Rapids community and contribute their knowledge in many fields. The community includes architects, physicians, dentists, psychologists, writers, attorneys, business owners, and teachers and college faculty members.[128] Latvians are known as hard workers, both honest and trustworthy.

Other Enclaves

Although the Latvians in Michigan are concentrated in the Kalamazoo, Detroit, and Grand Rapids areas, as already discussed, there are a few who live in the Upper Peninsula and in northern Michigan. There are several families in the Grand Haven area as well as in Ann Arbor (often these families participate in the larger gatherings in the Detroit area, although they also have their own group gatherings and social events). Several families settled in northern Indiana, and they participate in the Kalamazoo community's social events. Families that settled in the Toledo, Ohio, area participate in the larger Detroit community gatherings.

The Saginaw/Bay City/Midland area was home to about five hundred Latvian immigrants in the early 1950s. Two families settled in this area in the late 1940s (H. Dīnvalds and A. Ronis) and thus began the "chain migration" to this area. The majority of the first immigrants to the area found work at the General Motors plants. On June 18, 1950, the Saginaw Latvian Club was founded, and on February 1, 1951, it received nonprofit status, becoming the "Latvian Club of Saginaw." This organization served as the focal point for the newly arrived families; it included a choir, a folk dancing group, a ladies' auxiliary, a school, sports groups, and other activities. The various Latvian communities in the Midwest shared their cultural legacy by traveling to other cities to give concerts, present plays, and give lectures. Under the wing of the Latvian Club a church was purchased (Lutheran) that still serves the community today. There have never been enough members to support a full-time minister in the community, and thus a minister from Detroit or Kalamazoo is asked to hold services.[129]

As previously mentioned, General Motors employed the majority of the early immigrants to the Saginaw/Bay City/Midland area. Today, most of these early community members have retired, and many of their children have moved to larger cities for education and employment. A few are still employed by GM, Dow, Dow Corning, and various other businesses. Although the community's numbers have dwindled, those who live in the area find a sense of belonging and preserve their cultural identity by organizing and attending ladies' handicraft meetings, church services, choir practices and concerts, and various social gatherings. Again, the Latvians have added to the larger community and work as engineers, as project managers, and as editors for the local newspaper, among other fields.[130]

The greater Lansing area also has a sizable number of Latvians. Again, the first immigrants to the area arrived in the late 1940s and early 1950s. The focal point of the community has always been the Lutheran congregation, the first church service having been held in 1951. Reverend Jānis Turks, from Kalamazoo, served as the minister for forty-two years, holding services one Sunday afternoon every month. Since there were not enough members to purchase a church, the congregation has, from the beginning, rented the University Lutheran church for a nominal fee.

In order to preserve the Latvian language and culture in the community, it was important for the immigrant children to maintain the language, so a school was needed. It began by having the children meet an hour before the monthly church service, but eventually began to meet weekly at a private home.[131] Eventually, several families began to take their children to the larger Latvian schools, held on Saturday mornings, in Detroit or Grand Rapids. The children would have to get up very early every Saturday and leave around 7:30 A.M., in order to arrive on time for the 9 A.M.school opening. As the population of school-aged children grew, the community decided in 1983 to reestablish a local Saturday school. Again the University Lutheran Church was a generous sponsor and allowed the use of their facilities. Guidelines for the curriculum were obtained from the American Latvian Association and approximately fifteen students attended and graduated. The school closed in May 1991.

A sports division has been active in organizing volleyball leagues and the present, ever popular golf tournaments. Also, in the 1970s and 1980s there were monthly social gatherings held in private homes,

The Lansing Latvian Folk dancing group Pirmais Solis. Photo by S. Meija.

usually on Friday evenings. People would share their travel experiences and show slides. Latvian films would be shown, and visitors from other Latvian communities would present lectures.

Several years ago, there were many Latvian professionals who worked in the Lansing downtown area, and they began to meet on a regular basis for lunch (the lunch bunch!).[132] The purpose was to keep the language alive and also maintain friendly ties with others in the area. Many of these professionals have now retired, and in the place of the lunch bunch is the "Latvian Happy Hour," which includes the same core group of people, with new additions, who again meet monthly either in local restaurants or private homes. This active group also works as an "unofficial" host to researchers, scientists, emergency response teams, and military personal who are visiting the area from Latvia. The local Latvians help with transportation, host dinners, organize picnics, and generally help visitors from Latvia in any way that they can.[133]

The State Government of Michigan has been an active employer of members of the Lansing Latvian community. Furthermore, many community members work at Michigan State University, as support staff and as professors and researchers.[134] For example, Dr. Māris Āboliņš, Michigan State University's high-energy physicist, was part of a team that helped "build the equipment and analyze the data that ultimately revealed the existence of the Top quark."[135] Furthermore, Dr. Āboliņš is now turning to the next stage of high-energy physics: finding the source of nonzero mass at the new Biomedical and Physical Building.[136]

Other Latvians in the community include attorneys, principals and vice principals, builders, librarians, teachers, physicians and members of a variety of other white-collar positions.[137]

"Little Latvia"

No discussion of Latvians in Michigan would be complete without looking at the founding and contribution of the Latvian Center in Three Rivers, on the shores of Long Lake, in Fabius Township ("Garezers" translated is "long lake"). Since its founding in the mid-1960s it has been a focal point of Latvian culture and activity for all Latvians, offering activities, events, and gatherings for all ages.

In 1963 a Latvian minister, Rev. V. Vārsbergs, had a congregation in Constantine, not far from Three Rivers. He heard that a Girl Scout camp, "The Lone Tree Camp" was for sale and thought it would be an ideal spot to develop a camp under the direction of the Midwestern Latvian congregations. A number of meetings were held the following year with representatives from Detroit, Chicago, Grand Rapids, and Kalamazoo Lutheran churches. After much discussion, the land was purchased for $181,400. On May 23, 1965, the Latvian Center "Garezers" was officially opened.[138] The center is a nonprofit organization governed by a board of directors with several officials at the helm, including the chairman of the board, the president, and various division leaders. It is funded by the purchase of stock certificates by various Latvian organizations; private individuals cannot hold stocks. On May 23, 1987, after the stockholders meeting, it was proclaimed that the mortgage had been paid off and the property carried no debt. "Garezers" cannot subsist financially on the income from high school and camp participants and rentals; thus there is always a need to create fund-raisers to help balance the budget and pay workers' salaries.

The parcel of land consists of 170 acres with 2,500 feet of frontage on Long Lake. The area is divided into several sections, including a

The Latvian Center Garezers high school procession going to their graduation ceremony. Photo by S. Meija.

children's camp, a high school area, a rental area (Dzintari), and an outdoor amphitheater (Dziesmu leja). Each of these areas has a specific purpose and function. For example, the camp area has five groups of cabins in a lovely wooded area, an open-air church and altar, a kitchen and eating area, a small store, an activity building with dormitory rooms for teachers, various maintenance buildings, an arts and crafts building, and a main office. In 1965 when the land was purchased there were few existing structures, but over the years many buildings have been built to house the high school students and create classrooms, a museum containing paintings, sculptures, jewelry, folk costume displays and so on, as well as other structures.

The center serves as a focal point for Latvians in the Midwest as well as other parts of the United States and Canada. In the winter, activity is at a minimum, with several scout camps and private functions being the only activities. In the summer the activity explodes, and the center becomes a hub of social interaction. The children's camp is held in three two-week sessions, the last two-week period being for children who do not speak Latvian but wish to learn. Activities are the same as in any summer camp, but only Latvian is spoken and the curriculum includes instruction in singing, folk dancing, religion, and other aspects

Two young girls in folk costumes at an outdoor celebration (St. John's day). Photo by S. Meija.

of Latvian culture. There are also a newly developed middle school and a very popular high school (GVV; Garezera Vasaras Vidusskola) on the grounds. On July 4, 1965, when Garezers first opened, there were 92 children in the summer camp and 10 in the high school.[139] In 1979 there were 214 students at the high school and 175 in the summer camp. In 1981, there were 212 in the high school and 195 in the summer camp.[140] The numbers dwindled in the 1990s but are again moving upward.

The high school is in session for six weeks. All instruction is done in Latvian, and the goal is to create a total immersion in the language and culture. Classes are held in the mornings, and after lunch the students can participate in various arts, crafts, and sporting activities. After dinner there is a study hall, which is followed by an organized evening activity. Students are taught history, geography, religion, writing, literature, and about the cultural heritage of Latvia. The school follows the curriculum developed by the American Latvian Association for high schools. Furthermore, all students participate in folk dancing and in the choir. The school is organized and administered by a director hired by the Garezers board of directors. Students are housed in dormitories and classrooms that have been built with contributions and

Instilling Cultural Heritage

A typical experience with the Latvian summer high school is exemplified by the recollections of one parent:

We had coaxed our son into the car, but he was adamant that he would not attend the first year at the Latvian summer high school (GVV) in Three Rivers, Michigan. When we arrived, I had to register him but he would not leave the car. He got out only when he saw his peers staring at him through the window. He called every night the first two weeks, begging me to pick him up.

In order to get him to attend the second summer I had to bribe him with a new bicycle. Again, the drive was difficult, but his new present would await him when he returned after six weeks.

The third summer was much better. He did not complain and even packed his own bags. I noticed he even took along a few magazines and disallowed items. The plan was to attack the girls' dormitories with toothpaste and squirt guns.

When I picked him up after the six weeks, he begged to spend one more night in Garezers, so he could have some final moments with his friends. On our trip home, he made a calendar with the date circled as to when he could return to the Latvian High School the next summer. We had not been home more than three days when letters began arriving, and the telephone began ringing incessantly. He had a difficult time adjusting to his American high school and his friends that fall.

The fourth summer my son asked if we could go to Garezers a few days early, before school started, because he wanted to spend time with a few friends who were vacationing with their families by the lake. The anticipation and excitement in getting ready for this final summer was incredible. He was packed and ready to go two weeks before our scheduled departure. He begged for my husband to drive faster, so he could be one of the first ones to arrive. At the end of the six weeks there was a graduation ceremony, a church service by candlelight in the outdoor church, and a presentation of folk dancing and singing. At the ceremony, all the graduates were in their folk costumes, tears were flowing, and some were even sobbing. The time had come to end their beautiful, fulfilling time of being immersed in their Latvian cultural heritage. The friendships made would last forever.

Our son is now married and has two small children. When I mention his days at the Latvian high school, he responds that "I shall send my children there. They will attend the summer camp and then the high school." He says that those were the best times of his teenage years.

Young children playing in Dzintari, a lakefront section of the Latvian Center Garezers, near Three Rivers, Michigan. Photo by S. Meija.

donations. The Latvian community sees this endeavor as a tremendous success, for it indoctrinates first and second generations with a nationalistic pride and a desire to maintain their cultural and ethnic roots.

Another important area of the center is the section by Long Lake called "Dzintari" (Amber). The purpose of this area is to support social interaction by people of all ages. There are a number of trailers there that belong to private individuals, who pay a yearly rental fee. There are a variety of lodging and rental options in the area, and many choose to camp in tents on the beach. There is a pavilion, which is a meeting place for friends and can be rented for private occasions. Families spend their vacations in this area, often when one or more children are attending the camp or the high school. Canoes and sailboats can be rented and there is a special pier for those who need to dock their motorized boats. There is a great influx of people during a weekend in the first part of August. There is an organized golf outing, where the participants play at a local golf course and in the evening have a social gathering in the pavilion. One can buy food at the food stand specifically organized for this weekend. Also, volleyball tournaments are held. On Saturday most of the high school students organize teams

A Place in My Heart

One middle-aged Latvian woman recounts her experiences at the Latvian Cultural Center, typical of the experiences of many Latvians from Michigan and around the country:

When I was fifteen years old the Latvian Center Garezers was purchased. The high school was to begin that summer, but I was asked to work as a camp counselor for the many children. I loved that summer in the woods, swimming and working with the small children.

When I was nineteen I saw my future husband swimming in the lake. We were married several years later. When my first child was two weeks old, we camped in a tent by the water. When my second child came, I spent several weeks during the summer in our tent with the two toddlers. When the third child came, we moved into a trailer. There we spent about eight weeks each summer for the next twenty four summers. My children attended the camp and graduated from the high school. I spent many summers pushing a stroller on the walkway. Soon, my children will be doing the same, raising their children to love the Latvian tradition and culture.

and play; on Sunday those eighteen and over play in a tournament on seven courts. People come from all parts of the United States and Canada for this event. It is heartwarming to see people of all ages come together. Those from the older generation sit in the shade, conversing with friends and watching the activities. The younger generation swim, sing, and becoming reacquainted. Grandparents and young mothers push strollers on the walkway.

Garezers also houses a weekly endeavor in August called "3 × 3" ("three times three"). In 1981 Dr. Liga Ruperts from Grand Rapids felt that a weekly gathering should be held that would offer cultural enrichment for all generations of Latvians. The participants in these gatherings range in age from tiny infants to those well into their eighties. Speakers, lecturers, and instructors offer workshops in journalism, teacher preparation, folklore, literature, cooking, various arts and

Latvian summer camp Garezers high school students singing in the outdoor church. Photo by S. Meija.

crafts, political discussion groups, and folk dancing. Participants can choose several workshops to attend. Children are provided with their own activities and are divided into the younger (0 to 5 years old) and the older (6 to 12 years old) groups. Evening activities include folk songs by a campfire and various lectures and discussion groups. All participants are housed at the center, and meals are taken together.

Every few years a Mini Song Festival (Dziesmu Dienas) is organized. The organizers send out a collection of songs to the Midwestern Latvian choirs, who learn the songs during the winter months. During the Song Festival weekend, a large choir practice is held with singers from all choirs, and a concert is given in the evening. In addition, there is a folk dancing exhibition, jewelry can be purchased, and smaller social gatherings take place. Again, this creates the opportunity for cultural revival and social interaction for Latvians throughout the United States and Canada.

While the Latvian Center Garezers provides cultural and social benefits to the Latvian community, the center also contributes to the local economy. During the summer months, when there is a great influx

Latvian Center Garezers high school graduation. Photo by S. Meija.

of people for the various social gatherings, the high school, and the camp, there is a discernible increase in economic revenue for local merchants in Three Rivers. Also, the camp pays taxes to the county and uses local craftsmen and service workers for maintenance and upkeep. More than forty Latvians have purchased homes on Long Lake and various surrounding lakes.

The local community is further strengthened by the adjacent Latvia subdivision, which has permanent homes. In the spring of 1967 the Latvian Lutheran Church of Christ in Detroit purchased farmland along Lucas Road. In September of that same year, the parish proclaimed a "Declaration of Covenants and Restrictions," which listed all of the rules and regulations pertaining to streets, plots, building codes, and the like.[141] A few years later another parcel of land was purchased a short distance from the first tract of land. Currently, there are over 167 individual lots in the subdivision, with many year-round homes already inhabited. The homeowners association represents the subdivision members on matters concerning property taxes, road conditions, and maintenance of the Common Park and pavilion. Again, the Latvian Center Garezers has brought new members to the Three Rivers community and surrounding area.

Mrs. M. Paudrups, a longtime teacher at the summer high school at Latvian Center Garezers. Photo by Mrs. E. Berzins.

This brings us to the end of our examination of how Latvians immigrated to Michigan, and where they settled and established their roots. It is clear that the Latvians are one of the many ethnic groups that enrich Michigan's culture. They are a "tile" that helps to form the state's vivid cultural mosaic.

The Relationship between Michigan and Latvia Today

The Michigan National Guard can be seen as the most vivid example of a personal and professional bond between Latvia and Michigan, with the sponsorship of the Latvian National Armed Forces (Zemes Sargi). The U.S. National Guard Bureau developed the concept of the State Partnership Program (SPP) in 1992 in response to the many stark political, socioeconomic, and military changes occurring in Central and Eastern Europe at the beginning of the 1990s. The State Partnership Program established a working relationship between the United States and selected states in the newly emerging democracies of the former Warsaw Pact and Soviet Republic countries. There are now twenty partnerships between the United States and countries of the former Soviet Union.[142]

The Michigan partnership with Latvia was established in July 1993 and is one of the most active State Partnership Programs within the United States European Command-Joint Contact Team Program Area of Operations. This relationship between the Michigan National Guard and the Latvian National Armed Forces has been instrumental in enabling Latvia "to gain stability [and] transition to a parliamentary democracy and continues to influence the military professionalism and NATO integration goals of Latvia." The Michigan National Guard has participated in over 220 bilateral activities that have directly influenced the professional development of over eight hundred Latvian soldiers and airmen.[143]

When Michigan volunteered to become a partnership state, the adjunct general committed the personnel and resources to make the program successful.[144] Under the terms of the partnership, the Michigan National Guard provides a representative who is stationed in Latvia as well as a state partnership coordinator who conducts daily activities in Latvia. The National Guard also sends subject matter experts (logistics and defense experts, management specialists, and others) to Latvia in support of the "Zemes Sargu" recruitment, training and development. They conduct briefings on United States military methods, systems, and standards. Timely events such as the NCO Career Path, Enlisted Personnel Management, and NCO Roles and Responsibilities influenced the fledging development of the Latvian NCO Academy. The Michigan National Guard also provided events targeted for senior leadership, staffs, and the National Defense Academy as they sought to refine the nature and structure of the Latvian armed forces in preparation for NATO consideration.[145]

In addition, the state supports regular visits by various personnel from the Latvian National Armed Forces to Michigan in order to allow them to directly observe various military functions. The visiting Latvians are taken to a variety of Army and Air Force bases for observations and briefings on the various activities, assignments, and duties of U.S. military personnel. During these visits, the local Latvian community, usually the Lansing contingency, organizes social gatherings to help make the military personnel's stay more enjoyable.

On an invitation from the United States ambassador to Latvia to participate in Riga's 800th anniversary celebration, the Michigan National Guard sent the 126th Army Band to Latvia. The band wasted no time in establishing a rapport with the Latvian National Armed Forces and with the Latvian people. Within hours of its arrival, the band conducted rehearsals with the Latvian National Armed Forces Staff Band. During their eight-day visit, the 126th Army Band conducted concerts with community bands in three towns. These concerts were open to the public, and one concert in Tukums was primarily for children

Former President of Latvia Guntis Ulmanis (fourth from left) after flying an F16 at Selfridge Air Force Base. President Ulmanis was a guest of the Michigan National Guard. Photo provided by Dr. J. Pone.

from a local rehabilitation center and orphanage. Additionally, the band conducted combined concerts with the Staff Band and Latvian Navy Band in formal celebrations for Riga's 800th anniversary. I had occasion to be at the Freedom Monument in the center of Riga during this celebration and heard the band perform and saw General Stump place a wreath at the base of the monument.[146] This was a glowing example of how Michigan has supported a new country's struggle to regain stability after so many years under foreign domination. Upon the band's return, the civic community donated a handicap-accessible bus to a children's rehabilitation center in Riga that had never before had transportation for the disabled children who attended the school. Furthermore, the National Guard has been instrumental in supporting agencies and groups throughout Latvia with monetary and clothing donations.[147]

The future promises continued and increased partnership between the Michigan National Guard and the Latvian armed forces. Beginning in March 2002, Michigan resourced a bilateral affairs officer within the Office of Defense Cooperation in the U.S. Embassy in Latvia. With

Latvia's acceptance into NATO, the structure supporting the relationship might change slightly, but the philosophy of support will remain the same. "The personal and professional bonds established over almost a decade of partnership between both militaries and communities has enriched both Latvia and Michigan."[148]

Former governor John Engler was a major supporter of the relationship between Michigan and Latvia. This can be seen in the press release issued by the Office of the President of Latvia on September 9, 2002, on the occasion of Governor Engler's visit:

> State President Vaira Vīķe-Feiberga met the Governor of the U.S. State of Michigan John Engler today and awarded him the Three Star Order of the second rank.
>
> When presenting the order, the President stressed the Governor's role and contribution to creating active co-operation between Latvia and the State of Michigan in the areas of education and environment as well as to supporting the growth of the Latvian Armed Forces.
>
> The Governor passed greetings from the U.S. President George W. Bush to the President of Latvia together with a rather appreciative evaluation of her speech in the U.N. General Assembly this autumn.
>
> During the meeting both parties agreed that good basis had been laid for expanding the contacts between the higher education institutions of Latvia and Michigan as well as for devoting more attention to the growth of economic contacts.
>
> Regarding the expected NATO summit in Prague, John Engler stressed that he supported faster admission of Latvia to NATO and wanted to be among the first who would congratulate the country after the possible NATO resolution on the issue in November. John Engler is an influential Republican representative and the most experienced of the U.S. governors, as he has been holding the position since 1990. Latvia and the State of Michigan have enjoyed long-term co-operation in the areas of defense, education, agriculture and environmental protection. The Governor has promoted and supported establishing the Partnership Program of Latvia with the State of Michigan as well as inviting Latvia to join NATO and signing the Charter on the U.S. and Baltic Partnership. Besides he has promoted

the exchange of the delegations of business people between Latvia and the USA as well as student exchange between both countries.[149]

The relationship between the populations of Michigan and Latvia does not stop with the state government support. Every Latvian community in Michigan, no matter what size, supports individuals, groups, agencies, and schools in need with clothing, monetary donations, or actual hands-on assistance in Latvia. Every Latvian congregation in Michigan has at least one sister congregation in Latvia to whom they send various forms of assistance. For example, the Lutheran congregation in Grand Rapids has three sister congregations in Latvia whom they support: The Ledurgas Church, St. Katrīnas in Vilkene, and Saulkrastu-Pēterupes Church.[150] Furthermore, they support several schools and a state social agency in Riga that offers assistance to homeless children.[151] The Saginaw Latvian Club sends books to schools and libraries in Latvia. They give financial aid to families in need either directly or through the American Latvian Association's relief programs. In addition, they give financial support to the restoration of a cemetery (Lesternes Brāļu Kapi) as well the Occupation Museum in Riga, which provides a vivid and gruesome recreation of how the Latvian peoples were brought to servitude and near annihilation. Some individuals have taken on personal projects, such as asking for donations, organizing fund-raisers, and spending several months at a time helping to rebuild a rural church.

There are numerous individuals who go to Latvia to work as consultants and help medical establishments, schools, the government, environmental agencies, and other organizations upgrade their standards and learn new techniques. There is no master list of individuals who offer assistance in Latvia; thus the size and scope of aid to Latvia is difficult to gauge. Physicians have sent textbooks and medical equipment, and people from the business communities have donated countless reference materials, textbooks, and computers to the University of Latvia and other educational agencies. Michigan State University and other state universities sponsor researchers from Latvia who want to further studies in their field.

Further support is tirelessly offered by the Michigan chapters of the Latvian Welfare Association (Daugavas Vanagi). For example, the

Grand Rapids chapter has organized countless fund-raisers and collected over twenty thousand dollars, which was donated to the
Michigan National Guard, who in turn dispersed the funds to families
in need in Latvia.[152] They sent financial support to various relief agencies and schools and collected books, shoes, and medicine, which were
then shipped as assistance for the needy and war veterans. Also, they
supported the restoration of the Freedom Monument, the Occupation
Museum, and various cemetery and church restoration projects. (See
appendix 8 for more information on the Latvian Welfare Association.)

Homeward Bound?

Previous chapters have traced Latvian immigration to Michigan beginning in the late 1940s. In Michigan, Latvians created communities, organizations, congregations, schools, and camps but also integrated in the larger community. The youngest of the original immigrants would now be about fifty years old, if they came to this country as infants; the oldest would be in their nineties. There is now a first and second generation of Latvian Americans. When these immigrants first came to America, their plan was that this would be only a temporary sojourn. In their new country they would work to preserve the language, culture, and traditions of their ancestors until it was possible for them to return to their homeland.

In 1991 Latvia regained independence, but where are the droves of expatriates flocking back to their homeland? Many did return to Latvia to offer guidance and assistance in their various fields, yet they returned to their established homes in the United States when this job was finished. A few individuals did return to Latvia to establish a new life and reclaim their homes (most often these were retired people or those from the younger generation who had finished their education here), yet the expected exodus did not occur.

One can only speculate why this did not happen. First, Latvians from Michigan have created new lives here. Homes have been purchased, children have been educated, a certain lifestyle has been attained by many, and most have established themselves in secure jobs. Many now find it difficult to liquidate their assets, sell their homes, give up lucrative jobs, and move to a different lifestyle and standard of living.

Second, there might be a divide between the two Latvian cultures. For almost fifty years those who remained in the homeland were subjugated under the Soviet way of life. Indoctrination into the Communist mentality was a primary goal. All aspects of educating the populace were infiltrated with communist ideology. Nationalism was denounced and forbidden. Only secretly could people pursue and propagate their culture and heritage. Daily survival was supreme under the harsh economic conditions. Conversely, during this same time, the Latvian immigrants in Michigan did not come to a land of "milk and honey" but had to work hard and often reeducate themselves. The difference was that there was opportunity and the chance for improvement. The Latvians in America established their own social structure but also had to integrate into the greater social environment; hence it is inconceivable that the Latvians in America would not become "westernized" or "Americanized," just as their counterparts in Latvia were "sovietized." Hence, a divide was created, and none is to blame, only history. Perceptions, mindset, and generational awareness add to the divide, but an ethnic and cultural seed will be seen sprouting in the near future. Each year the gap will become smaller and there will be more and more things in common between the two segments.

These speculations lead to questions about the future. The thrust and goal of the first Latvian immigrants was to preserve their language and culture; this is no longer necessary because now there is a free mother country. Will this produce greater assimilation and the eventual loss of Latvian culture in Michigan? Is there no longer a need to preserve the Latvian heritage and pass it on to future generations? If one wants to be a "real" Latvian, shouldn't one move to Latvia? Will there be a greater influx of those now living in Latvia to the United States? It would be interesting to compare, in about ten or fifteen years, the social interactions, cultural and ethnic zeal, and nationalistic pride of Latvian immigrants to those of other ethnic groups such as the Irish, Finnish, and Indians

The continuance of the Latvian culture in Michigan is in the hands of future generations; it will depend upon their zeal and willingness to work to maintain their heritage. The future will reveal to us how this will unfold.

Additional Information about Latvia

Written Resources

The American Latvian Association has many books available in Latvian and English. To get a list, contact: ALA apgada, 5648 Susan Avenue, Kalamazoo, MI 49048, or e-mail *dace.copeland@wmich.edu.*

Books available in English include Latvian/English dictionaries, cookbooks, children's books, novels, and historical works.

Internet Resources

There is a wealth of information, shopping opportunities, current articles, Latvian newspapers in English, travel information, political updates, and the like available on the World Wide Web. Following is a listing of related websites:

- *www.Latviansonline.com:* countless links to Latvian-related areas of interest
- *www.balticship.com:* jewelry, foods, books, and so on that can be ordered and sent to anywhere in the world
- *www.usembassy.lv:* the United States Embassy in Latvia
- *www.am.gov.lv/en/:* the foreign ministry

- *www.latvia-usa.org:* the Latvian Embassy in Washington, D.C.
- *www.alja.org:* the American Latvian Youth Association
- *www.alausa.org:* the American Latvian Association
- *www.jbanc.org:* Joint Baltic American National Committee
- *www.latvians.com:* information on Latvian folk history
- *www.garezers.org:* Latvian Center at Three Rivers, Michigan (Garezers)
- *BirutaP3@aol.com:* tours to Latvia (Biruta's Tours)
- *www.krikisjewelers.com:* Krikis Jewelers in Wisconsin
- *www.balticlinks.com:* Baltic links
- *www.balticexplorere.com:* Baltic Explorer search engine
- *www.diena.lv:* Daily Latvian newspaper
- *www.nra.lv:* Latvian newspaper (*Neatkarīgā Rīta Avīze*)
- *http://progr.radio.org.lv/realaud/index_a.htm:* Latvian radio
- *http://www.ltv.lv:* Latvian television
- *www.binet.lv/café:* the Internet café
- *www.latvians.com:* Latvian community
- *www.gallery.lv:* Latnet art gallery
- *www.balticinema.lv:* Baltic films
- *www.sports.lv:* sports in Latvia
- *www.lbl.lv:* Latvian Basketball information
- *www.search.lv:* search engine for Latvia
- *www.aldaris.riga.lv:* Aldaris Brewing Company of Latvia
- *www.gramata21.lv:* Virtual Encyclopedia
- *www.davana.lv:* Abrakadabra (online shopping)
- *www.ltv.lv/panorama_www/index.html:* Panorama (News about Latvia)
- *www.pbla.lv:* World Federation of Free Latvians
- *www.zagat.com:* ZAGAT restaurant guide
- *http://:* University of Wisconsin's Baltic studies program (offers one-semester programs in English in Latvia)
- *www.latviatravel.com:* Latvian Tourism Development Agency

Travel to Latvia

Anyone wishing to travel to Latvia can access any of the preceding websites for more information. Most major airlines fly to Riga, the capitol, and several cruise ships tour the Baltic sea and dock in Riga. Contact your local travel agent for more information.

Latvian Language

Together with Lithuanian, Latvian makes up the East Baltic branch of the Baltic language family. It has been spoken in approximately the same area (the geopolitical boundaries of Latvia) since at least the thirteenth century. Influences on the Latvian language have come from three sources: the Western Finnic, Germanic, and Slavic languages. After the Latvian people's ancestors (Semigallian, Selian, and Latgalian speakers) came into contact with Finno-Ugric languages, their language developed some notable distinctions from its earlier state, including placing the word stress on the first syllable, loss of short and shortening of long end vowels, development of low form vowel (e), and regressive vowel harmony. At some point Latvian lost the instrumental case ending, which is still active in Lithuanian.

The first preserved written texts in Latvian are from the sixteenth century. These are exclusively religious texts written by non-Latvians in the "Gothic" script, which are inadequate for representing the Latvian sounds. Also, the syntax and phraseology were literally transferred from

All information in this appendix is taken from Lalita Muizniece, "Latvian," in *Facts about the World's Languages: An Encyclopedia of the World's Major Languages, Past and Present*, edited by Jane Garry and Carl Rubino (New York: H. W. Wilson Company, 2001), 417–20. Many thanks to the author.

the German language, resulting in fairly strange renderings. The translation of the Bible (1685-94), both the New and Old Testaments, by a number of mainly German pastors, edited by Ernst Gluck (1652-1705), exerted considerable influence on later texts. Some of the German syntactic patterns, established in this publication, lingered in the Latvian written language until the twentieth century.

During the period of "National Awakening" in the middle of the nineteenth century, Latvians themselves took charge of the development of their language, bringing it up to the standards of other modern languages. To accomplish this, many new terms were coined, mainly by a derivation process from existing Latvian words. As a part of this process, borrowings from the classical languages were brought into Latvian and many unneeded Germanisms were taken out. Modern Latvian was consciously forged out of three sources: folklore, especially the language of the folk songs; former written texts; and new coinage and borrowings. To prove that Latvian was capable of expressing any idea, Juris Alunans (1832-64) published a collection of original and translated poetry, "Dziesminas" (Songs) in 1864. This little book is considered to be a milestone marking the beginning of the modern Latvian language.

Around the turn of the century and thereafter, Latvian linguists, notably K. Mulenbachs and J. Endzeliņš, studied the Latvian language extensively and published a large number of articles and several major works (grammars and dictionaries). They laid the foundations for the present Standard Latvian or modern literary language.

Orthography and Basic Phonology

Latvian uses the Latin alphabet, supplemented by three diacritical marks: a macron over a vowel to indicate length, and a cedilla under, or a wedge over, a consonant to indicate a palatal position or articulation. In Latvian, length is phonemic. All Latvian vowels can appear long or short; long (a, e, i, u) are indicated by a macron over the vowel letter, but (o) is generally written without the macron: o.

Basic Morphology

Latvian nouns consist of three parts; the noun stem, a thematic vowel, and a declension ending provides information about case, gender, and number. Latvian has five cases, nominative, accusative, dative, genitive, and locative. An additional case, the vocative, is used for animate objects only. There are two genders, masculine and feminine, and two numbers, singular and plural. Adjectives agree with the nouns they modify in gender, number, and case:

Maz-s	Bern-s	
Small (NOM.M.SG)	*child* (NOM.M.SG)	"a small child"

Maz-I	Berni-i	
Small (NOM.M.PL)	*child* (NOM.M.PL)	"small children"

There are two sets of adjective endings, one for definite nouns and one for indefinite nouns.

Biez-ā grāmat-a	"a thick book" (NOM.F.SG)
Biez-ā grāmat-a	"the thick book" (NOM.F.SG)
Biez-ai grāmat-ai	"to a thick book" (DAT.F.SG)
Biez-ajai grāmat-ai	"to the thick book" (DAT.F.SG)

Basic Syntax

The basic word order in Latvian sentences with nominal objects is SVO; with pronominal objects, SOV. In most sentences, the subject is in the nominative case and the direct object is in the accusative:

Es	redz-u	māt-i	
I (SG.NOM)	*see* (I SG)	*mother* (SG.ACC)	"I see (my) mother"

Māt-e	man-i	redz	
Mother (SG.NOM)	*I* (SG.ACC)	*see* (3)	"Mother sees me"

Common Words

man: vīrietis	*woman:* sieviete	*water:* ūdens
sun: saule	*three:* trīs	*fish:* zivis
big: liels	*long:* garš	*small:* mazs
yes: yā	*no:* ne	*good:* labs
bird: putns	*dog:* suns	*tree:* koks

Example Sentences

Ir rudens.	*It's autumn.*
Mēs esam šeit.	*We are here.*
Nāc mājās.	*Come home!*

The phonology, morphology, and syntax of the Latvian language have changed little since the first written records of the thirteenth century. To keep the language from becoming an international jargon, a terminology committee in the Latvian Academy of Sciences that consults with scientists and technicians is at work trying to find appropriate new coinages or derivations in the fields of science and technology.

Learning Latvian

If you wish to learn the Latvian Language there are several avenues you could follow. There are audiotapes available for self-instruction, as well as a number of books for the individual learner. Many of the larger Latvian communities throughout the United States and Canada also have individuals who would be willing to give instruction. For more information, contact the Berlitz Language School, the American Latvian Association, or get information on the Internet.

Appendix 3

Latvian Food

L atvian cooking can be divided into country cooking and city cooking, to which now has been added a dash of cosmopolitan flavor. . . .

The country cooking is simple but hearty fare, although rather bland in flavor for some palates. Typically, the tropical countries of the world use many sharp and hot spices, while northern countries of Europe use very little of them, relying more on the natural flavors of their products. It seems that everything grown in the Baltic region has a more pronounced flavor. This may be due to the climate, short summers with cool sun but with long daylight hours ripen things slowly, developing flavors to their fullness. Added flavorings in Latvian dishes come from cream, dill weed, caraway, onions, nuts, seeds and other homegrown things. Exotic spices are usually added to special dishes on special occasions.

Lots of dairy foods, cooked cereals, bacon, meats and potatoes, and the ever present dark rye bread with fresh butter and cottage cheese, are all very substantial, simple and tasty for the hard working Latvian farmer. Latvia exported large amounts of dairy, meat and fish products to many countries in prewar Europe.

The information in this appendix is taken from *Latvian Cooking* (Hamilton, Ont.: Ladies Auxiliary of the Latvian Relief Society of Canada, 1985). Many thanks to the authors.

City cooking, in general, is more influenced by the cuisines of our neighboring countries than country cooking. By incorporating other tastes and food traditions and adapting them to our own, a certain style developed that can be called the Cuisine of Riga. In restaurants, besides truly Latvian dishes, one could also order Scandinavian herring salad, German "Koeningsberger klops," Russian borsht, to name just a few.

Riga, during the years of Latvia's independence, was very proud to have one of the largest produce markets in all Europe, second only to the famous Les Halles in Paris. Five huge halls (former hangars) displayed mountains of food, each food category having its own hall; farm and garden produce, meats, fish, dairy products and breads.

Latvians in the free world try to keep their old traditions alive by celebrating traditional holidays, organizing worldwide song festivals, printing Latvian books, organizing schools, etc.; among these traditions is also the tradition of food. If not in everyday life, the traditional country dishes are still served at special events to reaffirm our adherence to our roots.

Leafy Green Salad

Fresh garden vegetable salads are usually served with sour cream, buttermilk, or yogurt dressing. Sour cream seems to be the most often used substance in Latvian cooking. However, not every salad that is mixed with sour cream automatically becomes a Latvian salad!

    ½ cup (or more) sour cream (if cream is thick, dilute with
        buttermilk or milk)
    pinch of sugar and salt to taste
    ½ tsp. lemon juice (optional)
    2 Tbsp. chopped green onions or chives
    1 Tbsp. chopped dill weed
    1 large head leaf lettuce or Boston (never iceberg or Romaine)

Mix sour cream with the seasonings and chopped greens. Wash and dry lettuce; tear into pieces. Place half of the lettuce in a salad bowl; set the other half aside. Pour the dressing on top and mix very gently. Place bowl in refrigerator for 15 minutes to blend tastes. The salad will be rather limp, but this is important for it to acquire its specific leafy-green taste. When you are ready to serve, add the remaining half of the lettuce, mix very lightly, and serve at once.

At this point, the salad is ready, but as a variation you can add some sliced cucumber and a handful of sliced radishes for color. However, never add tomatoes, green peppers, celery, or other greens. The salad can be garnished with rounds of sliced hard-boiled egg.

Tomatoes, radishes, and cucumbers are most often made into salads all by themselves.

Herring/Potato Salad, called "Rassol"

Salad

> 1 cup diced cooked chicken
> 1 cup diced cooked pork or beef
> 1 cup diced boiled potatoes
> 1 cup diced hard-boiled eggs
> 2 cups diced pickled beets
> 1 cup diced peeled fresh apples
> 1 cup diced salt-herring
> 1 cup diced dill pickles

Dressing

> 1 cup salad dressing
> 1 cup sour cream
> 1 Tbsp. mustard, prepared

Combine all salad ingredients, add mixed salad dressing, toss, and chill for at least two hours.

Pork Aspic (Gallerts)

No cold buffet at a Latvian party would be complete without some kind of meat aspic. In everyday life, too, there's often an aspic stored in the refrigerator, to be used as lunch or a quick snack, accompanied by black bread, vinegar, mustard, or horseradish.

3 fresh pork hocks
4 1-lb. pieces of very lean pork (shoulder or tenderloin)
salt to taste
1 bay leaf
5 peppercorns
1 celery stalk
1 carrot (thinly sliced)
1 tomato
1 onion
several sprigs green parsley
½ envelope gelatin

Wash and dry pork hocks thoroughly. In a large saucepan, cover all meat with cold water and bring to boil. Skim well. Reserve the parsley and gelatin, add the rest of the ingredients, and simmer slowly for about 2 hours or until the meat is tender and falls from the bones. Remove from heat; strain. Return stock to saucepan. Place meat on a large platter and allow to cool completely.

Rinse a few small or large dishes (round or square, whichever shape you would like to unmold) with cold water. Chop cooked carrots together with parsley and sprinkle on the bottom of the dishes. Dice completely cooled meats, including pork skin, into small pieces, removing excess fat and any bones. Place meat into bowls, to about half full.

If you have too much stock, reduce it by boiling to the quantity required for covering the meat. Dissolve gelatin in the stock completely. Now cover the meat with stock until dishes are full. Store in refrigerator until jellied; then cover dishes with foil or plastic.

When ready to present, unmold aspic onto platter and decorate if you wish. Slice to serve as needed. May be served with a sprinkle of vinegar or a dab of mustard or horseradish.

Frikadelle Soup (Meatball Soup)

"Man does not live by bread alone. He must have soup! It is said that you can make a good soup even from a broomstick if the seasonings are right!" (*Latvian Cooking,* Hamilton, Ontario: Ladies Auxiliary of the Latvian Relief Society of Canada, 1985).

Soup

1½ quarts stock, or water with bouillon cubes

2 to 3 potatoes, diced

parsley and celery

1 onion, whole, or 1 leek, chopped

2 carrots, diced

(you can add any other vegetables, diced)

Sauté vegetables in a bit of butter for a few minutes, then add liquids and continue to cook slowly until done.

Frikadelle Mix

½ lb. very lean ground beef

1 egg

1 Tbsp. bread crumbs

1 Tbsp. sour cream

1 onion, finely chopped

salt and pepper to taste

Mix all ingredients well. Form little round balls and slowly roll into simmering soup. Remove the onion. Boil on low until the meatballs are fully cooked (cooking time depends on how large the meatballs are). Garnish with fresh chopped parsley.

Brown Sweet Sauerkraut

"Sauerkraut plays at least a minor role in the cooking of most countries where cabbage is grown, but in the Latvian cuisine it is a star. It is served suitably cooked and seasoned as an accompaniment to meat dishes like pork roast, sausages, dark meat fowl, and game.

The technique of making sauerkraut has hardly changed since it was recorded by the ancient Romans, who seem to have acquired it from the Orient. It consists of adding salt to shredded cabbage and then allowing it to ferment. Europeans forgot the method until the conquering Tartar hordes, bringing it from China, reintroduced it to Austria in the thirteenth century. The Austrians gave sauerkraut its name (literally "sour plant/cabbage") and passed it along to their neighbors. Before the era of fast transport and good refrigeration, sauerkraut was an important source of vitamin C in the winter when fresh greens were not available. *Note:* Fresh salad is never served with sauerkraut.

> 1 large can (about 28 oz.) fine, German type wine sauerkraut
> 1 Tbsp. lard or bacon drippings (or substitute butter or margarine)
> ½ tsp. caraway seeds
> a pinch of pepper
> 2 apples, diced, or 1 small can applesauce
> 1 bay leaf
> 1 onion, chopped fine (optional)
> 3 to 4 Tbsp. brown sugar

Drain sauerkraut only if it is too salty; otherwise use with its own liquid. Heat lard in a large saucepan. Take a handful of sauerkraut and squeeze dry. Put in hot lard and fry until sauerkraut has brown edges. Add remainder of sauerkraut, other ingredients starting with 2 tablespoons of brown sugar. Add water to just barely cover sauerkraut. Bring to a boil; lower heat and simmer for about 2 hours, stirring occasionally. Add more sugar, if needed, gradually, while sauerkraut is cooking, tasting often. Sauerkraut should be pleasantly sweet-sour, but not too sweet. Recipe can be doubled.

Note: The more sauerkraut is reheated the better it gets. Therefore, it is better to cook it a day before that special dinner. This will also mean that your house will not smell as strongly of sauerkraut on the day of your meal.

"Kotlettes" (Latvian Meat Patties)

This is probably the most popular ground meat dish in Latvia.

1 onion, chopped
½ lb. bacon, diced fine
1 lb. ground lean beef
1½ lb. ground pork
1 cup breadcrumbs
salt and pepper to taste
2 eggs
1 tsp. potato flour or cornstarch
2 Tbsp. sour cream
bread crumbs for coating

Sauté onion with bacon until transparent. Reserve bread crumbs for coating, and in a large bowl mix all other ingredients together. If mixture is too dry, add a bit of milk or stock. Mixture should be soft and pliable, and should hold together.

With wet hands, roll mixture into golf-size balls. On a wooden board, roll balls in breadcrumbs and, with the blunt edge of a knife, flatten them down slightly, making a criss-cross pattern on both sides.

Heat butter or oil in the bacon drippings in frying pan. Over medium heat, fry patties on both sides until brown.

Arrange in a single layer on a heated platter and garnish with greens. Serve very hot with a cream sauce or a mild creamy tomato sauce. Traditionally "kotlettes" are served with boiled or mashed potatoes, diced carrots, and freshly shelled peas in a creamy sauce, with a green salad or dill pickles on the side.

Custard Pudding (Bubberts)

3 eggs, separated
3 Tbsp. sugar, divided
4 Tbsp. flour (or ½ cup cream of wheat)
3 cups milk

¼ tsp. salt
½ tsp. vanilla

Note: When using cream of wheat, sprinkle over cold milk. Bring to a
boil, stirring constantly. Reduce heat to low and simmer 5 minutes or
longer. Follow the rest of the recipe.

Mix egg yolks with 2 tablespoons of the sugar. Beat egg whites with
the remaining 1 tablespoon of sugar until stiff. Mix flour with a little
cold milk to form a paste. Add more milk to thin it to the consistency of
heavy cream. In a heavy saucepan bring the rest of the milk and salt to
a boil. Gradually add the flour mixture, stirring constantly. Boil for one
minute. Add egg yolk mixture. Boil for one minute longer. Remove from
heat and add vanilla. Fold in stiffly beaten egg whites. Spoon into desert
dishes. Serve with your favorite fruit sauce, fresh or frozen cranberries,
currants, rhubarb, strawberries, or raspberries. Makes 6 servings.

Cranberry Ķīssēls

Ķīssēls are fruit "soups," thickened with starch and known all around
the Baltic shores. The English have something similar, called the
Flummery. A cold, refreshing ķīssēls is just about the most popular
summertime dessert in Latvia. A ķīssēl can be prepared from almost
any fruit or berry. The berries can be used whole, diced, or strained
through a sieve.

½ lb. cranberries, or more
1 quart water
sugar, according to taste
2 Tbsp. potato starch (more potent) or cornstarch, mixed
    with cold water

Rinse cranberries and put to boil in 1 quart water. When all berries have
burst, strain and force through a sieve. Retain liquid and pulp; discard
skins. Reheat the juice while mixing in sugar and tasting. Slowly add the
starch, stirring and carefully watching thickness. It should be like thick
syrup, but not like glue. Pour hot ķīssēl in a deep bowl or serving dishes,

and sprinkle sugar on top to prevent a skin from forming. Cover and cool.

Serve cold with milk or table cream poured on top, or dabs of whipping cream. Ķīssēl makes a nice sauce for creamy white pudding.

When using other berries, the proportion is about 1 lb. berries to a quart of water. Sweeten according to taste. It is up to you whether you want a clear or pulpy dessert.

Red currants and other very juicy berries should be first passed through a sieve, in order to obtain the juice. Then the skins should be cooked with water, strained, and the skins discarded. Finally this juice should be added to the uncooked juice. This way the ķīssēl retains the fresh fruit taste.

Strawberries, raspberries, and even blueberries first should be divided in half. Cook one half and make the ķīssēl, then add the other, uncooked half (slightly mashed with sugar) to it, so it tastes like fresh berries.

This is one of my family's favorite desserts. I use rhubarb and apple chunks, and add a large box of strawberry or raspberry gelatin, dried prunes, raisins, and sugar to taste.

Midsummer Night's Cheese (Jāņu siers)

In ancient times many peoples of the world observed the summer solstice as an important mythical event. In northern Europe this tradition carries on, and the Midsummer Night, which is the shortest night of the year, is still celebrated with great exuberance. The ancient Latvians believed that this night belonged to the demigod Jānis, who came to visit earthlings in summers' beauty and bounty. On this occasion, a potent ale was brewed and a big wheel of Jānis cheese was served with it. It may well be that this recipe is one of the oldest in Europe. In the Christian era June 24 is observed as St. John the Baptist's Day.

6 eggs

4 lbs. dry curd cottage cheese (This often has to be ordered from the grocer. If not available, use large curd cottage cheese and decrease milk by ½ cup).

3 liters 2% milk (3 quarts 6 oz.)

1 Tbsp. caraway seeds

1 liter buttermilk (1 quart 2 oz.)

½ cup butter

1 tsp. salt

Cheesecloth or other porous cloth.

Thoroughly mix the eggs with the cottage cheese. Bring milk and caraway seeds to a boil; add cheese mixture and bring to boil. Add buttermilk and continue heating and stirring until whey separates from curds
and the liquid turns to a watery yellow color.

Dampen the cloth, spread it over a sieve in a large bowl, and drain
the curds, squeezing out as much liquid as possible. Return curds to
saucepan, add butter and salt, and mix well with a wooden spoon over
low heat.

Put mixture back into cheesecloth and squeeze out remaining liquid. Shape the cheese (in the cloth) into a flat wheel. Place between two
plates, tightening the cloth and spreading it over the wheel, and put a
heavy weight on top. Place in refrigerator overnight to drain and ripen.·

When serving, slice cheese with a sharp knife. Eat as is or spread
with sweet butter and sprinkle with a bit of salt. This type of cheese is
never eaten in a sandwich.

Latvian Bacon Rolls or Piragi

Pastry

½ tsp. sugar

½ cup warm water

2 envelopes dry yeast

2 cups whole milk, scalded

2 tsp. salt

½ cup oil

2 eggs, slightly beaten

½ cup sour cream

about 6 cups all-purpose flour

2 Tbsps.

Bacon Filling

2 lbs. lean bacon, diced very fine

1 medium onion, chopped fine

ground pepper and salt to taste, but mixture should not
   be too bland

In a hot pan, stir-fry the bacon filling mixture quickly for 5 minutes but do not let too much fat separate. Remove separated fat. Cool mixture quickly in refrigerator. (*Authors note:* Some people add diced Spam or lean, cooked ham to the mixture.)

To prepare yeast: In a small bowl, mix sugar with water; sprinkle yeast on top; set aside in a warm place for 10 minutes. Yeast should bubble up to double the size.

Meanwhile, scald milk and put in a large mixing bowl. Add salt, sugar, and oil and stir. Mix eggs with sour cream in a separate bowl. When milk is cooled to lukewarm, add egg mixture, then add yeast mixture and 2 cups of the flour. Beat thoroughly with wooden spoon or electric mixer. Add another cup of flour and continue beating.

Remove beaters and continue mixing with a spoon or dough hook. Add almost all the rest of flour. The dough will be quite stiff but still sticky. When the dough begins to leave the sides of the bowl, turn it out onto a lightly floured pastry board. Work enough flour into the dough so that it can be handled without sticking to hands or the board. Knead dough with the heels of your hands for 5 to 10 minutes, slapping the ball forcibly down on the board a few times.

Place ball into a greased bowl; grease the top of the dough and cover with a plastic sheet. Place in a warm spot to rise, about 1½ hours, or until doubled.

Punch dough down, and take half out onto a floured board. Roll into a long strand, about 20 inches long. With a knife, cut into even pieces, about 1 inch each. Repeat with the other half of dough. With your hands, roll and flatten each piece into a pattie, large enough to hold 1 teaspoon of filling in the middle. Add filling. Fold the edges up and pinch closely together. Place the rolls on a greased cookie sheet with the pinched seams down. Bend rolls slightly into a crescent shape (optional). Before putting into the oven, brush tops with slightly beaten egg and stab with a fork to release steam. Bake in a preheated 400° oven for about 12 to 15 minutes until golden light brown. Makes about 80.

Author's note: Pīrāgi can be made ahead of time, put in freezer bags, and frozen. When ready to use, put on cookie sheet, sprinkle with water, and warm in oven.

Excerpt from the Report of Crimea Conference

The Premier of the Union of Soviet Socialist Republics, the Prime Minister of the United Kingdom, and the President of the United States of America have consulted with each other in the common interests of the peoples of their countries and those of liberated Europe. They jointly declare their mutual agreement to concert during the temporary period of instability in liberated Europe the policies of their three governments in assisting the peoples liberated from the domination of Nazi Germany and the peoples of the former Axis satellite states of Europe to solve by democratic means their pressing political and economic problems.

The establishment of order in Europe and the rebuilding of national economic life must be achieved by processes which will enable the liberated peoples to destroy the last vestiges of Nazism and Fascism and to create democratic institutions of their own choice. This is a principle of the Atlantic Charter—the right of all peoples to choose the form of government under which they will live—*the restoration of sovereign*

This appendix is an excerpt, "Declaration on Liberated Europe," from the Report of Crimea Conference (commonly called the Yalta Conference), February 11, 1945 (taken from the *United Nations Primer*, Sigrid Arne [New York: Farrar and Rinehart, 1945]). **89** *rights and self-government to those peoples who have been forcibly deprived of them by the aggressor nations* [my italics].

To foster the conditions in which the liberated peoples may exercise these rights, the three governments will jointly assist the people in any European liberated state of former Axis satellite state in Europe where in their judgment conditions require (A) to establish conditions of internal peace; (B) to carry out emergency measures for the relief of distressed peoples; (C) to form interim governmental authorities broadly representative of all democratic elements in the population and pledged to the earliest possible establishment through free elections of governments responsive to the will of the people; and (D) to facilitate where necessary the holding of such elections.

The three governments will consult the other United Nations and provisional authorities or other governments in Europe when matters of direct interest to them are under consideration.

When, in the opinion of the three governments, conditions in any European liberated state or any former Axis satellite state in Europe make such action necessary, they will immediately consult together on the measures necessary to discharge the joint responsibilities set forth in this declaration.

By this declaration we reaffirm our faith in the principles of the Atlantic Charter, our pledge in the declaration by the United Nations, and our determination to build in cooperation with other peace-loving nations world order under law, dedicated to peace, security, freedom and general well-being of all mankind.

In issuing this declaration, the three powers express the hope that the Provisional Government of the French republic may be associated with them in the procedure suggested.

Appendix 5

Latvian Folk Songs (Dainas)

Germans dominated the Baltics for over seven hundred years. Historians allude to the harsh life the peasants lived, but since they did not leave their own historical records, their voice has been absent from history. The Latvian folk songs, or "Dainas," show the oppression the peasants suffered and the modes of resistance they employed.

These lyrical folk songs typically consist of two unrhymed couplets. The meter in most is trochaic (four accented syllables to each line), or less frequently dactylic (two accented syllables per line). They are either recited or sung. Few "Dainas" have been translated into English, as it is possible to translate them only thematically. In translation some rhyming elements are lost.

The current president of Latvia, Dr. Vaira Vīķe-Freiberga, has done extensive study on the various aspects of the Dainas, and especially on the sun motif (see her work entitled *Linguistics and Poetics of Latvian Folk Songs: Essays in Honour of the Sesquicentennial of the Birth of Kr. Barons*). As she points out:

This appendix is an excerpt from Maruta Lietiņa Ray, "Recovering the Voice of the Oppressed: Master, Slave, and Serf in the Baltic Provinces," *Journal of Baltic Studies* 34, no. 1 (Spring 2003): 1–21.

The songs survived, immune to those kinds of changes that make the
stuff of written history. Whatever the dates of battles fought and whatever the names of the kings who won or lost them, the land remained
fundamentally the same, worked by the force of horse and man.
Customs changed only slowly and gradually, and the songs changed
slowly along with them, adding new layers as time went on, but always
preserving deeper layers which went back to remote antiquity. (Ray,
"Recovering the Voice of the Oppressed")

Krišjānis Valdemars (1825-91) initiated the first attempt to collect
the folk songs. Transcribers traveled across Latvia to collect the songs
as well as additional folklore material. One should remember that this
was oral history, and nothing had been written down before; now they
were beginning to be transcribed, and the informants and the locations
where the songs were heard were also noted. By 1912 a total of 217,996
Dainas had been collected. Krišjānis Barons (1835-1923) joined the project in 1878 and compiled and edited the material. The collecting of
Dainas continued during Latvia's independence and by 1938 they had
collected a total of 2,308,000 of these lyric folk songs.

Together . . . [the Dainas] described all the major events in a peasant's
life: birth, child rearing, courtship, marriage, weddings, married life,
death, and burial; the tasks men and women and children were called
upon to perform in an agrarian or a seafaring society; their relationships to nature, animals and plants; their religious practices, and their
magical spells and charms. The Dainas, however, are not only a cultural archive of peasant society. They are also a vehicle for transmit-
ting the peasant's moral philosophy, his attitude towards the world he
encountered, and his evaluation of it. (Ray, "Recovering the Voice of
the Oppressed")

The Dainas can be divided into several categories, one of which is a
description of the modes of oppression, both physical and psychological,
that the peasants endured under the German landed gentry. Another
examines the types of resistance the peasants practiced in order to preserve their identity as human beings and to affirm their values.

For example, the "muiža," or the German estate, is a symbol of the Latvian peasants' drudgery, slavery, and suffering, and the serfs knew that their hard work was what made the farm successful. A number of the Dainas dealt with this fact:

A grand "muiz˘a" on the hilltop, what made it so grand?
It is the great effort of the workers,
And the shouting of the overseer. (31409)

Another example:

Ozolmuiz˘a, muiz˘a of slaves
I wish you would sing down into the depths of hell.
The young weep upon arrival, the old weep upon departure,
The Iecava (river) flows by full of the tears of the servants. (31418)

The serfs were at the mercy of the owner and could be subjected to physical abuse:

Harsh masters flogged the people with nine pairs of canes;
With nine pairs of canes, and tied to the stake by the hair. (52591)

The master was making my plowman dance at the end of his cane.
For now, master, he is in your power and you can torture him.
But just you wait: the God of Thunder
Will catapult you into the lowest depths of hell. (31319)

Another, more pleasant Daina:

Kas to teica, tas meloja,	*[Whoever said it, lied,*
Kā saulīte naktī guļ:	*That the sun sleeps at night;*
Vai saulīte tur uzleca,	*Does the sun rise*
Kur vakar norietēja?	*Where it set yesterday?]*

Appendix 6

Speech by Latvian President Vaira Vīķe-Freiberga

Mr. Secretary General,
Excellencies,
Heads of State and Government,

On behalf of the Republic of Latvia and its people I thank all the heads of state and government of the NATO member countries for [the] courage to make the decision that they announced today. For us in Latvia it comes as a sign of international justice. It will put an end for once and for all [to] the last vestiges of the Second World War, to the last sequels of what started with the Molotov-Ribentrop pact in 1939, to the consequences of the decisions taken in Teheran and Yalta.

Latvia had lost its independence for a very long time, and it knows the meaning both of liberty and the loss of it. Latvia knows the meaning of security and the loss of it. And this is why being invited in an alliance that will ensure our security is a momentous moment that will be writ large in the history of our nation.

We would like to congratulate you on the wisdom of your decision.

This appendix is a speech given by the President of Latvia Vaira Vīķe-Freiberga at the NATO Summit in Prague during the meeting of NAC and the seven invited states, November 21, 2002. (Reprinted from *Latvian Dimensions* (Newsletter of the Latvian Association) 3 (2002): 9. **95**

You have taken a plunge, and you have put your faith in us, you have been guiding us and helping us along the path of reform that we have been undertaking. All of you sitting around this table in one way or another have pushed us, have encouraged us, and you have stood by our side as we have tried to recover from half a century of totalitarian rule, from half a century of oppression. We come from a very long way and we would like to thank you for having been at our side, for having been ready to shoulder us and to encourage us in all the difficult steps that we have been taking so far, in all the difficult steps that are still ahead of us. Because, of course, the road is but half done and we still have a process of ratification ahead of us. We thank you for your trust and we would like to . . . [assure] you that it has been well placed. We are committed to the same ideals that you are. We would like to enjoy the same liberties and freedoms that you have enjoyed for so long and that we have so recently recovered. We are ready to work as hard as we ever had to attain the same standards, the same levels and to make full contribution. And I think that this NATO summit can be summarized in one word—Hope. Hope for a better future both for those nations— all seven of us—who have received this historical invitation today but hope also for those nations for whom the door has not been closed, as it was for us; for those who have still to stand ready, and I think, will be encouraged by our progress, to continue their striving and their efforts, because they see that it can lead to the result that we all hope for.

We in Latvia would like to build our future on the rock of political certainty, not on the shifting sands of indecision. We do not want to be in some sort of gray zone of political uncertainty; we would like to enjoy the full sunshine of liberties and rights that NATO has been defending so long. We do not want to be left out in an outer darkness, and we would like to enjoy the full sunshine of liberties and rights that NATO has been defending so long. We do not want to be left out in an outer darkness, and we would not wish it to happen to any other nation who has expressed the desire to join those nations that hold the same values, that follow the same ideals, and that are ready for the same efforts and the same strivings. Our people have been tested in the fires of history; they have been tempered in the furnace of suffering and injustice. They know the meaning and the value of liberty. They know that it is worth every effort to support it, to maintain it, to stand for it and to fight for it. We make a solemn pledge and a commitment here today on this historical and solemn occasion that we will strive to our utmost to do our part to contribute not just to the strength of the Alliance but to do whatever needs to be done to create the world where justice and liberty are available to all.

Appendix 7

Excerpt from the *Boston Globe*

There was a long list of dignitaries in the hallways, conference rooms, and state dinners at last week's NATO summit who had done so much to usher Eastern Europe from its dark history into its brighter future. There was the feted host, the playwright and Czech president Vaclav Havel, who led the Velvet Revolution, sweeping out a Soviet-backed regime. On the fringe of the meeting, there was a quiet newspaper editor wearing a beat-up suede jacket named Adman Michnik, who spent years in communist jails for his role as an underground leader of Poland's Solidarity movement. But it was President Vaira Vīķe-Freiberga of Latvia—with a moving speech and her dramatic narrative of fleeing her country in World War II, only to return to it a half-century later into the Western alliance—who seemed to embody the history in the making at the gathering.

"Our people have been tested in the fires of history, and they have been tempered in the furnaces of suffering and injustice," Vīķe-Freiberga, 64, said Thursday in her speech. "They know the meaning

Reprinted from Charles M. Sennott and Brian Whitmore, "Latvia Shining Example for New NATO Nations," by Charles M. Sennott, Globe Staff, and Brian Whitmore, Globe Correspondent, *Boston Globe*, November 24, 2002, A32, as quoted in *Latvian Dimensions* (Newsletter of the American Latvian Association) 3 (2002).

and the value of liberty; and they know that it is worth every effort to support it, to maintain it, to stand for it, and to fight for it."

Senior White House officials said President Bush was profoundly moved by her words, and as she spoke without any prepared text before the other 25 heads of state, the room was still and the leaders listened.

The U.S. ambassador to the North Atlantic Treaty Organization, Nicholas Burns, said: "You could feel what she was saying. There was absolute silence in that room. President Bush was very moved by it, and I believe it was one of the finest speeches I have ever heard in Europe."

Thursday night, at the heads of state dinner, Vīķe-Freiberga was invited to sit at the head table with Bush, Havel, Prime Minister Tony Blair of Britain, and President Jacques Chirac of France.

Like neighboring countries Estonia and Lithuania, also invited to join NATO at the summit, Latvia had long been a historical stomping ground for Europe's great powers. In the twentieth century, the country fell victim to two of history's most murderous regimes; Hitler's Germany and Stalin's Soviet Union. And after the fall of the Soviet Union, they waited for a decade as Western powers, leery of offending Moscow, hesitated to invite them to join the alliance.

As president, Vīķe-Freiberga has had little patience for Moscow's objections to Latvia joining NATO. She said she would like Latvia to "get rid of the tag" of being called a "former Soviet country" forever. But she has also reached out to the country's large Russian minority.

As a young girl, Vīķe-Freiberga witnessed both the Russian and German invasions of her homeland, which she fled with her family in 1944 ahead of the advancing Red Army. Officials attending the NATO summit say her history, and that of her country, reflects the message of overcoming tyranny with hope they wished to convey at the two-day meeting in the Czech capital.

She has recounted vivid memories of her family's escape: an allied air raid, the loss of a six-month-old sister to pneumonia, and the sight of a girl who had been gang-raped and mutilated by Soviet soldiers. Her family first stayed in a disease-infested refugee camp in Germany, lived briefly in Morocco, and eventually settled in Toronto. Vīķe-Freiberga's first job was as a bank teller. She eventually earned a doctorate from McGill University and became a professor of psychology at the

University of Montreal. She returned to an independent Latvia in 1998 and won the country's presidency in June 1999.

"My personal history is with hundreds of millions who suffered a similar fate," she said Friday as the summit ended. "Millions have been submitted to the tyranny of totalitarian powers. And we have to remember that it happened here in Europe, in civilized Europe."

Daugavas Vanagi: The Latvian Welfare Association

The History of Daugavas Vanagi (DV)

The origins of the Dougavas Vanagi, hereby referred to as DV, organization may be traced to a British POW camp located in Belgium at the close of World War II. Former members of the Latvian Legion founded the DV organization in this POW camp on December 28, 1945. The organization's initial goals were to provide support to soldiers and their families.

Nearly 12,000 Latvians were interned in Allied POW camps; mainly those administered by the British in northern Germany. While many were scattered among numerous camps, some 12,000 were housed at the Zedelgem camp in Belgium, until their release in 1946. From its inception in late 1945 and 1946, the DV organizers were allowed to communicate with Latvians in other camps to help form a support network. Although the original membership was composed of former legionnaires, the founders of the DV organization hoped to eventually include all Latvians in the ranks of membership. After their release from POW camps, the soldiers were transferred to Displaced Persons camps, where they continued in their efforts to provide support and unity.

The information in this appendix is reprinted from the "Zinotajs" (the Kalamazoo area Latvian informational flyer), by Daugavas Vanagi, December 2002, 10.

Eventually, the Latvians left the Displaced Persons camps and moved to their new homes in England, Europe, Canada, South America, and the United States. The Daugavas Vanagi went with them.

The first DV chapter in the United States was founded on January 6, 1950, in New York. From that beginning, DV grew to encompass 22 chapters and 3 sections located throughout the United States, from coast to coast. Today, the DV has 2,552 members in the U.S. Unfortunately, the membership of the United States chapters has been steadily declining due to the effects of age on the American Latvian Community.

The United States DV organization (DV ASV) consists of seven departments, each of which is represented on the 12-person board of directors. The departments coordinate the work of the local chapters in each area (ideology, information/communications, women's auxiliary, culture, youth, welfare, and sports). A chairman heads the board.

Over the decades, the DV members perpetuated their mission to gather and unite Latvians for the preservation of the Latvian nation. For many years this was interpreted as a tireless struggle in defense of Latvia's right to freedom, which earned DV the eternal hate of the Soviet occupiers. DV has also striven to foster the education and involvement of young Latvians in the expatriate Latvian community, providing stipends to students and facilitating the work of Latvian schools, choirs, folk dance groups, theater troupes, sports teams, and various other cultural activities.

Notes

1. Jack Glazier, "Issues in Ethnicity," in *Ethnicity in Michigan: Issues and People* (East Lansing: Michigan State University Press, 2001), 3.
2. Ibid., 3.
3. Ibid., 13.
4. It is located in a temperate climatic zone, with the average summer temperature being 11°C at night and 23°C during the day. In January the temperatures range from –2 to 17°C.
5. Guntis Stamers, *Latvia Today* (Riga, Latvia: Latvian Institute of International Affairs, 1995), 15.
6. Ibid., 16.
7. Ibid.
8. Ibid.
9. Ibid.
10. Ibid., 17.
11. Ibid.
12. Ibid., 18.
13. Ibid.
14. Ibid.
15. Ibid., 19.
16. Ibid.

17. Ibid.

18. Ibid., 18.

19. Ibid., 20.

20. Ibid.

21. Ibid.

22. Ibid., 21.

23. Ibid.

24. Ibid., 23.

25. Ibid.

26. Ibid.

27. Ibid., 24.

28. Ibid.

29. Ibid., 25.

30. Ibid.

31. Ibid.

32. Ibid., 27.

33. Charles M. Sennott and Brian Whitemore. "Latvia Shining Example for New NATO Nations," *Boston Globe.* November 24, 2002, A32.

34. *Baltic Appeal to the United Nations.* "Batun President's Letter." Spring 2003, 1.

35. Quoted in Modris Eksteins, *Walking Since Daybreak; A Story of Eastern Europe, World War II and the Heart of Our Century.* New York: Houghton Mifflin Company, 1999, 115.

36. Ibid., 115.

37. Ibid.

38. Ibid., 116.

39. Ibid., 131.

40. Ibid., 165.

41. Ibid.

42. Ibid.

43. Ibid., 166.

44. Sigrid Arne, *United Nations Primer* (New York: Farrar and Rinehart, 1945), 94.

45. Ibid., 105.

46. Eksteins, *Walking Since Daybreak,* 112.

47. Ibid.

48. Marvin Klemme, *The Inside Story of UNRA: An Experience in Internationalism* (New York: Lifetime Editions, 1949), 1.

49. Ibid., 9. In 1938 the first agency was created to deal with the refugees—The Intergovernmental Committee on Refugees (IGCR). It was founded at the initiative of the United States, originally intended to deal with German and Austrian refugees from the Nazi regime, but eventually expanded (see Klemme, *Inside Story*, 13).

50. Tommie Sjoberg, *The Powers and the Persecuted: The Refugee Problem and the Intergovernmental Committee on Refugees (IGCR), 1938–1947* (Sweden: Lund University Press, 1991), 178.

51. Ibid., 224.

52. Ingūna Daukste-Silasproge, *Latviešu Literārā Dzīve un Latviešu Literatūra Bēgļu Gados Vācija 1944–1950* (Rīga, Latvia: Zinātne, 2002), 14.

53. Ibid., 16.

54. Daukste-Silasproge, *Latviešu*, 39–55.

55. Klemme, *Inside Story*, 246.

56. Ibid., 247.

57. It was interesting that when interviewing individuals about their experiences in displaced persons camps I found two very diverse opinions. Some stated that it was a pleasant and happy time; food and shelter was given and there was much time for cultural and social events. Conversely, there were those who looked upon this time as living in "rat-infested" squalor and feeling great anxiety about their unknown future.

58. Sjoberg, *Powers*, 210.

59. Ibid., 224.

60. J. Leja, "Kalamazoo," in *Atmiņu Taķa: 1950–2000,* ed. Vilis Miķelsons (Kalamazoo, Mich.: Kalamazoo Latviešu Biedriba, 2000), 60.

61. Ojārs Brūvers, *From War to Freedom: An Autobiography.* N.p., n.d., 70.

62. Ibid., 69.

63. Ibid.

64. Valda Lēvenšteins, "Ernests Brože Mūžībā" *Laiks,* July 1, 1994.

65. Leja, "Kalamazoo," 60.

66. Ibid.

67. Ibid.

68. Brūvers, *From War to Freedom*, 69.

69. Leja, "Kalamazoo," 61.

70. Ibid.

71. Vilis Miķelsons, "Kalamazū," in *Atmiņu Taķa: 1950–2000*, ed. Vilis Miķelsons (Kalamazoo: Kalamazoo Latviešu Biedrība, 2000), 38.

72. Ibid.

73. Krisjānis Brūveris, "Pirms 15 gadiem," in *Atmiņu Taķa: 1950–2000*, ed. Vilis Miķelsons (Kalamazoo: Kalamazoo Latviešu Biedrība, 2000), 7.

74. Ibid., 8.

75. Jekabs Grotens, "Kalamazū un Apkartnes Latviešu Biedrības 25. Gadi," in *Atmiņu Taķa: 1950–2000*, ed. Vilis Miķelsons (Kalamazoo: Kalamazoo Latviešu Biedrība, 2000), 12.

76. Miķelsons, "Kalamazū," 41.

77. Ibid.

78. Ibid., 20.

79. Ibid., 40.

80. Ibid.

81. Ibid., 41.

82. Lalita, Muižnieks, e-mail message to author, February 17, 2003.

83. "Rietrummičigānas Universitātes Latviešu Studiju Programa," May 1992, brochure.

84. Muižnieks, e-mail.

85. Ibid.

86. "Nāksim Visi Talkā," n.d., brochure.

87. Maira Bundža, Brochure about the Latvian Student Center, March 1990.

88. Muižnieks, e–mail.

89. Miķelsons, "Kalamazū," 42.

90. Ibid., 43.

91. Svētā Pāvila Latviešu Ev. Lut. Draudzes Detroitas Darbība, informal flyer, 9.

92. Ibid.

93. Ibid.

94. Ibid.

95. Ibid.

96. Ibid., 10.

97. Ibid.

98. Ibid., 9.

99. LAD/Latviešu Apvienība Detroitā, informal flyer, 10.

100. Ibid.

101. Dainis Rudzītis, "Detroitas Latviešu Sabiedriskā Un Nacionālpolitiskā Rosme 20 Gados," informal flyer, 16.

102. Ibid., 1.

103. Ibid.

104. Ibid.

105. Ibid., 17.

106. Ibid., 18.

107. Gundega Ozols, interview by author, (Lansing, Michigan, April 30, 2003.)

108. *www.Gunarbirkerts.com/biography*

109. *www.Gunarbirkerts.com/biography*

110. "Mana Debesu Zilie Amati," *Laiks*, October 19, 2002, 4.

111. Andris Ozols, e–mail, "Juris Upatnieks," May 7, 2003.

112. Gundega Ozols, interview.

113. Ibid.

114. Ibid.

115. Brūvers, *From War to Freedom*, 69.

116. Ibid.

117. Ibid., 10.

118. Andris Runka, "Ievadam," in *Grand Rapidu Latviešu Biedrības 50 gadi*, ed. Līga Gonzales, Ausma Linde, Ruta Puriņa, and Julieta Rumberga (Grand Rapids, Mich.: Grand Rapids Latvian Association, May 5, 2001), 4.

119. Ibid., 3.

120. Ibid.

121. Ibid., 5.

122. Ibid.

123. Ibid., 6.

124. "Grand Rapidu Latviešu Biedrības Sākums," 9.

125. Dr. Z. Zadvinskis, "Grand Rapidu Latviešu Katoļu Draudzes Loma Grand Rapidu Latviešu Biedrības Aktivitātes," in *Grand Rapidu Latviešu Beidrības 50 gadi*, ed. Li‾ga Gonzales, Ausma Linde, Ruta Puriņa, and Julieta Rumberga (Grand Rapids, Mich.: Grand Rapids Latvian Association, May 5, 2002), 58.

126. Dr. A. Ruperts, e-mail message to author, May 24, 2003.

127. Dr. L. Gonzales, e-mail message to author, March 16, 2003.

128. Dr. A. Ruperts, e-mail message to author, May 12, 2003.

129. Alfrēds Paeglis, "Speech for the 40th Anniversary for the Saginaw Latvian Club," (Saginaw, Michigan, October 21, 1990.)

130. Dainis Martinsons, e-mail message to author, May 27, 2003.

131. Paulis Kubuliņš, "50 Gadu Darbības Pārskats," 7.

132. Gundega Ozols, interview.

133. Ibid.

134. Ibid.

135. Andris Ozols, e-mail message to author, May 19, 2003.

136. Ibid.

137. Gundega Ozols, interview.

138. Dr. V. Medenis, "Garezera Attīstības Gaita," in *Garezers 50 Gados; 1965–1990*, ed. Dr. V. Medenis (Three Rivers, Mich.: Garezers, 1990), 14.

139. Ibid.

140. Tīdmanis, Arvīds, and V. Medenis. "Administrācija 25 gados," in *Garezers 25 Gados: 1965–1990*, ed. V. Medenis (Three Rivers, Mich.: Garezers, 1990), 27.

141. "Ciems Latvija; 25 Gadu Atcere," 2. Pamphlet.

142. Flyer. No author. Given by Major General Gordon Stump. May 14, 2002.

143. Ibid.

144. Ibid.

145. Ibid.

146. Ibid.

147. Ibid.

148. Ibid.

149. Press release, Office of the President of Latvia, September 21, 2002.

150. Ruperts, e-mail, May 24, 2003.

151. Ibid.

152. Maksis Jansons, letter to author, March 27, 2003.

For Further Reference

Arne, Sigrid. *United Nations Primer*. New York: Farrar and Rinehart, Inc., 1945.

Arnte, Biruta. *Latvian Price Reforms and Their Effects on the Production*. Ames, Iowa: Center for Agricultural and Rural Development, 1992.

Babris, Peter J. *Baltic Youth Under Communism*. Arlington Heights, Ill.: Research Publishers, 1967.

The Baltic Question: Latvia, a Case of Soviet Imperialism and Genocide. Why is the West Silent? The Canadian Committee for Human Rights in Latvia and Latvian section of Kitchener-Waterloo Black Ribbon Day Committee, 1987.

The Baltic States, a Reference Book. Riga: Latvian Encyclopedia Publishers, 1991.

Baumanis, Arturs, ed. and comp. *Latvian Poetry*. Augsburg: A. Baumanis, 1946.

Benton, Peggie. *Baltic Countdown: A Nation Vanishes*. London: Centrans Press, 1984.

Berzins, Alfreds. *The Two Faces of Co-Existence*. New York: Robert Speller and Sons, 1967.

Berzins, Alfreds. *The Unpunished Crime: A Case Study of Communist Takeover*. New York: Robert Speller and Sons, 1963.

Bilmanis, Alfreds. *The Baltic States in Post-War Europe*. Washington, D.C.: The Press Bureau of the Latvian Legation, 1943.

Bilmanis, Alfreds. *Dictionary of Events in Latvia*. Washington, D.C.: The Latvian Legation, 1946.

Bilmanis, Alfreds. *A History of Latvia.* Princeton, N.J.: Princeton University Press, 1951.

Bilmanis, Alfreds. *Latvia in the Making, 1918–1928 (ten Years of Independence.)* Riga: The Riga Times, 1928.

Blesse, A. *Illustrated Basic Latvian-English-German Dictionary.* Waverly, Iowa: Latvju Gramata, 1976.

Budina-Lazdina, Tereze. *Teach Yourself Latvian.* London: English Universities Press, 1996.

Clemens, Walter C., Jr. *Baltic Independence and Russian Empire.* New York: St. Martin's Press, 1991.

Comrades and Cameras: Photographs from Latvia and Other Soviet Republics, February 9 through April 28, 1991. Santa Barbara, Calif.: Santa Barbara Museum of Art, 1991.

Cullen, Robert. *Twilight of Empire; Inside the Crumbling Soviet Bloc.* New York: The Atlantic Monthly Press, 1991.

Dreifelds, Juris. *Latvia in Transition.* Cambridge, New York: Cambridge University Press, 1996.

Dreifelds, Juris, comp. *Baltic Studies: Facts for Students.* Mahwah, N.J.: Association for the Advancement of Baltic Studies, 1983.

Dukhanov, M., I. Feldmanis, and A. Stranga. *1939 - Latvia and the Year of Fateful Decisions.* Translated by Karlis Streips. Riga: University of Latvia, 1994.

Economic Development of Latvia. Riga: Ministry of Economy, Republic of Latvia, 1997.

Eglitis, Olgerts. *Nonviolent Action in the Liberation of Latvia.* Cambridge, Mass.: Albert Einstein Institution, 1993.

Ekis, Ludvigs. *The Truth about Bolshevik and Nazi Atrocities in Latvia.* Washington, D.C.: Press Bureau of the Latvian Legation, 1943.

Eksteins, Modris. *Walking Since Daybreak.* New York: Houghton Mifflin Company, 1999.

English-Latvian Dictionary; Anglu-Latviesu Vardnica, 2nd ed. Riga: Jana Seta, 1996.

Ezergailis, Andrew. *The Holocaust in Latvia, 1941–1944.* Riga: Historical Institute of Latvia; Washington, D.C.: United States Holocaust Memorial Museum, 1996.

Ezergailis, Andrew. *The Latvian Impact on the Bolshevik Revolution; the First Phase: September 1917 to April 1918.* Boulder, Colo.: East European

Monographs; New York: Columbia University Press, 1983.

Ezergailis, Andrew, ed. *The Latvian Legion: Heroes, Nazis, or Victims?: A Collection of Documents from OSS War-crimes Investigation Files, 1945-1950.* Riga: Historical Institute of Latvia, 1997.

Ezergailis, Inta M., ed. *Nostalgia and Beyond; Eleven Latvian Women Writers.* University Press of America, 1997.

Fennel, Trevor G. *A Grammar of Modern Latvian.* Vols. 1-3. The Hague, Paris, New York: Mouton, 1980.

Gerner, Kristian, and Stefan Hedlund. *The Baltic States and the End of the Soviet Empire.* New York: Routledge, 1993.

Gessner, Lynne. *Edge of Darkness.* New York: Walker, 1979.

Glazier, Jack. *Ethnicity in Michigan: Issues and People.* East Lansing, MI: Michigan State University Press, 2001.

Gordon, Frank. *Latvians and Jews Between Germany and Russia.* Translated by Vaiva Pukite and Janis Straubergs. Stockholm: Memento, 1990.

Hansen, Birthe, and Bertel Heurlin, eds. *The Baltic States in World Politics.* New York: St. Martin's Press, 1998.

Hough, William J. H., III. *The Annexation of the Baltic States and its Effect on the Development of Law Prohibiting Forcible Seizure of Territory.* Vol. 6, no. 2. New York: New York Law School Journal of International and Comparative Law, 1985.

Huggins, Edward. *Blue and Green Wonders and Other Latvian Tales, as told by Edward Huggins.* New York: Simon and Schuster, 1971.

Iwens, Sidney. *How Dark the Heavens: 1400 Days in the Grip of Nazi Terror.* New York: Shengold Publishers, 1990.

Jegers, Benjamins, ed. *Bibliography of Latvian Publications Published Outside Latvia, 1981–1991.* Stockholm and Riga: Daugava, 1995.

Kalnins, Ingrida, ed. *A Guide to the Baltic States.* Merifield, Va.: Inroads, 1990.

Karklis, Maruta, Liga Streips, and Laimonis Streips, comps. and eds. *The Latvians in America, 1640–1973: A Chronolgy and Fact Book.* New York: Oceana Publications, 1974.

Klemme, Marvin. *The Inside Story of UNRA.* New York: Lifetime Editions, 1949.

Krueger, Rudolf M. *The Krueger Memoir: Life After Death in the Soviet Union.* Huntington, W. Va.: Aegina Press, 1993.

Lacis, Vilis. *Towards New Shores; a novel.* Moscow: Foreign Languages Publishing House, 1959.

Langton, Jane. *The Hedgehog Boy: A Latvian Folktale.* New York: Harper and Row, 1985.

Lasmane, Valentine. *A Course in Modern Latvian.* Rockwille, Md.: Amerikas Latviesu Apvieniba, 1985.

Latvia between the Anvil and the Hammer. Washington, D.C.: The Latvian Legation, 1945.

Latvia in 1939–1942; Background, Bolshevik and Nazi Occupation, Hopes for Future. Washington, D.C.: Press Bureau of the Latvian Legation, 1942.

Latvia under German Occupation, 1941–1943. Washington, D.C.: Press Bureau of the Latvian Legation, 1943.

Latvia under Soviet Occupation. Toronto: Latvian National Federation of Canada, 1951.

Latvijas Republikas Satversme (Constitution of the Republic of Latvia). Riga: Tiesiskas Informacijas Centrs, 1997.

Lesins, Knuts. *The Wine of Eternity; Short Stories from the Latvian.* Translated by Ruth Speirs and Haralds Kundzins. St. Paul, Minn.: University of Minnesota Press, 1957.

Lieven, Anatol. *The Baltic Revolution; Estonia, Latvia, Lithuania and the Path to Independence.* New Haven, Conn.: Yale University Press, 1993.

Mangulis, Visvaldis. *Latvia in the Wars of the 20th Century.* Princeton Junction, N.J.: Cognition Books, 1983.

Manning, Clarence. *The Forgotten Republics.* New York: Philosophical Library, 1952.

Memo to America: The DP Story. The Final Report of the United States Displaced Persons Commission. Washington, D.C.: US Government Printing Office, 1952.

Millers, Antonina. *Latvian Language: Grammar, Vocabulary, Excercises for the Use of Students.* West Menlo Park, Calif.: Echo Publishers, 1979.

Moseley, Christopher. *Colloquial Latvian: A Complete Language Course.* London; New York: Routledge, 1996.

Nefedova, Inara. *Masterpieces of Latvian Painting.* Translated by Maija Oginta. Riga: Liesma, 1988.

Nesaule, Agate. *A Woman in Amber.* New York: Soho, 1995.

"New Latvian Fiction." *The Review of Contemporary Fiction* 18, no. 1 (Spring 1998).

Plakans, Andrejs. *Historical Dictionary of Latvia.* Lanham, Md.: Scarecrow Press, 1997.

Plakans, Andrejs. *The Latvians: a Short History.* Stanford, Calif.: Hoover Institute Press, Stanford University, 1995.

Plaudis, Arturs, ed. *The Dead Accuse: Collection of Letters From Behind the Iron Curtain.* Park Orchards, Australia: JAJM Fund, 1984.

Pojate, G. and M. Sosare. *Latvian for Foreigners.* Riga, 1995.

Punga, Inara A. and William Hourger *A Guide to Latvia.* Old Saybrook, Conn.: The Globe Pequot Press, 1995.

Punga, Inara, ed. *Guide to Latvia.* Chalfont St. Peter, Bucks, U.K.: Bradt Publications; Old Saybrook, Conn.: Globe Pequot Press, 1995.

Ramonis, Val. *Baltic States vs. the Russian Empire; 1,000 Years of Struggle for Freedom.* Lemont, Ill.: Baltech Publishing, 1991.

Raskevics, J. and J. Vejs. *English-Latvian Phraseological Dictionary.* Riga: Jumava, 1993.

The Republic of Latvia. Riga: Latvian Encyclopaedia Publishers, 1995.

Scandinavian & Baltic Europe on a Shoestring. Hawthorn, Australia: Lonely Planet Publications, 1993.

Schneider, Gertrude. *Journey Into Terror: Story of the Riga Ghetto.* New York: Ark House, 1979.

Silde, Adolfs. *The Profits of Slavery; Baltic Forced Laborers and Deportees Under Stalin and Khrushcev.* Translated by Valdemars Kreicbergs. Stockholm: Latvian National Foundation in Scandinavia, 1958.

Spekke, Arnolds. *History of Latvia: An Outline.* Stockholm: M. Goppers, 1951.

Skulme, Dzemma and Juris Dimiters. *Contemporary Latvian Art.* Sewickley, Pa.: International Images, 1986.

Survival Latvian; a Traveller's Phrase Book. Riga: Jumava, 1993.

Svabe, Arveds. *Genocide in the Baltic States.* Stockholm: Latvian National Fund in the Scandinavian Countries, 1952.

Svabe, Arveds. *The Story of Latvia; A Historical Survey.* Stockholm: Latvian National Fund, 1949.

Sveics, Vilnis. *How Stalin Got the Baltic States; a Search for Historic Truth.* Jersey City, N.J.: Jersey City State College, 1991.

Talonen, Jonko. *Church Under the Pressure of Stalinism. The development of the status and activities of Soviet Latvian Evangelical Lutheran Church during 1944–1950.* Published by The Historical Society of Northern Finland, Rovaniemi, 1997.

These Names Accuse: Nominal list of Latvians deported to Soviet Russia in 1940–41:

With Supplementary List. 2nd ed. Stockholm: Latvian National Foundation in cooperation with the World Federation of Free Latvians, 1982.

Trapenciere, Ilze and Sandra Kalnina, eds. *Fragments of Reality: Insights on Women in a Changing Society: Proceedings of the Latvian Academy of Sciences Institute of Philosophy and Sociology.* Riga: Vaga Pub, 1992.

Turkina, E. *Latvian-English Dictionary.* Riga: Avots, 1982.

U, Ruta. *Dear God, I wanted to Live.* Translated by Rita Liepa. Brooklyn, N.Y.: Gramatu Draugs, 1987.

Upitis, Lizbeth. *Latvian Mittens: Traditional Designs and Techniques.* Translated by V. Berzina-Baltina. St. Paul, Minn.: Dos Tejedoras, 1981.

Vairogs, Dainis. *Latvian Deportations 1940 - Present.* Rockville, Md.: World Federation of Free Latvians.

Vike-Freiberga, Vaira. *Linguistics and Poetics of Latvian Folk Songs.* Kingston: McGill-Queen's University Press, 1989.

Von Rauch, Georg. *The Baltic States: Estonia, Latvia, Lithuania. The Years of Independence, 1917–1940.* London: C. Hurst & Co., 1974.

Weyman, Mark. *DP, Europe's Displaced Persons, 1945–1951.* Philadelphia: The Balch Institute Press, 1989.

Who's Who in Latvia. Riga: Publishing House of Valery Belokon, 1996.

Zarina, Ina, ed. *News About Women in Latvia.* Riga: Latvian Women Studies and Information Center, 1994.

Ziedonis, Arvids, William L. Winter, Mardu Valgemae, eds. *Baltic History.* Columbus: Ohio State University, Association for the Advancement of Baltic Studies, 1974.

Index